The
Happy
European

Laetitia de Warren is a television presenter and journalist who was born in Rome of French parents, learnt English in Zimbabwe at the age of five, and currently lives in Compiègne, just north of Paris. She is the author of *Setting up in France* and contributed to the *Daily Telegraph's* Buying a Property in France. Her journalistic work includes writing about Britain for French publications, and editing *Alliance*, the Franco-British publication of the Alliance Francaise.

The Happy European

A survival guide to the EC

Laetitia de Warren

Dedication

This book is dedicated to my 340 million countrymen in the European Community

First published in 1992
by Charles Letts & Co. Ltd,
Letts of London House,
Parkgate Road,
London SW11 4NQ

ISBN 1 85238 191 4

A CIP catalogue record for this book is available from the British Library

'Letts' is a registered trademark of Charles Letts & Co. Ltd
Printed in the United Kingdom

Contents

Acknowledgements

A substantial part of the information contained in this book has been obtained thanks to the London and Paris offices of the Commission of the European Community. The author would like to stress the warm welcome and helping hand extended by the relevant press offices, headed by Lindsay Armstrong in Paris and Robert Elphick in London.

The figures and statistics dotted here and there were obtained through Eurostat, Eurobarometre and Euroscopie.

This book is designed to contribute to public debate on European integration. Neither the Commission of the European Community nor any person acting on its behalf is responsible for the use made of the information it contains. This book is not an official publication of the EC.

Every effort has been made to ensure accuracy at the time of going to press. However, events in Europe are moving fast and some information may have become outdated after publication. No responsibility for this can be accepted by the author or the publisher.

Introduction

WHAT'S IN IT FOR US?

Let's face it. Europe is here to stay. So we might as well make the most of it. In the next ten years, the European Community as we know it – or think we know it – will be undergoing as many changes, if not more, as it has known since it first saw the light of day in Rome all those thirty-five years ago. What these changes will be is anybody's guess – will they bring about an enlarged European economic community gathering to itself the States of Eastern and Northern Europe, or a European Federation, or a European Confederation, or a simple Free Trade Association? Only time and the will of Europeans will tell.

But if Europeans want to be capable of deciding how they are going to be united – or even if they want to be united – their first preoccupation must surely be to understand what a United Europe means, on the basis of the structures that already exist and the institutions that, willy-nilly, are even now influencing their lives.

This book is not a guide for European businessmen – there are already scores of those and businessmen have no excuse for not being the best-informed of EC citizens. It is not a political pamphlet, trying to convert anti-Europeans into rabid pro-Europeans, or vice versa. Nor is the author a specialist in European business, institutions or affairs.

The aim of this book is to try and stop the average European citizen being messed around by all those who take advantage of his ignorance concerning most EC activities to further their own aims, whatever they may be, pushing him into accepting preconceived opinions on something he actually knows very little about.

It is the work of one of those average European citizens who, tired of being told what to think about the European Community while never being told simply what it's about, decided to find out what's actually in it for all of us, people of Europe, on a practical, understandable, everyday basis.

And, believe it or not, one of the first things one discovers when starting to explore the workings of the Community is that all the necessary information is there for those who take the trouble to look for it. The problem is that there is, in fact, a little too much of it – there are hundreds and hundreds of books, brochures, articles, essays, interviews, radio and TV programmes, to say nothing of the thousands of people directly involved; far too much for any one person to absorb and clarify, unless they have the time and opportunity to concentrate on that one problem to the exclusion of anything else, for as long as it takes.

Which is where being a journalist can come in useful. After all, what is the role of a journalist if not to gather as much information as possible on a subject, from as many possible sources, try and understand what is important and what is irrelevant, and then put everything together in such a way that the problem becomes, hopefully, easier to understand?

As the author's only speciality is that of being a journalist, this book is first and foremost a quest for facts. On that basis others can form an opinion.

What is, really and truly, this Single Act which politicians keep quarrelling over, without telling us what it is made up of, whom it actually concerns or where it is leading to?

How does the European Community really function, who are the people that make it work, how did it all start, how much is it costing us and can we afford it?

These are some of the questions this book tries to answer, not so much by listing the thousands of figures and dates that specialists are always throwing at our heads, but by gathering the various threads of the European story and putting them together to see how they all lead to the Single Market, not only by 1 January 1993, but in the years to come.

Hopefully, by the time they reach the end of the book, readers will have realized that, beneath all those thousands of bits of information, news and opinions hurtling past our eyes all the time, there is, and has been, a coherence in the Community's actions and, most importantly, in its objectives – whether we approve of them or not.

Some of its decisions are already affecting us, some may not do so for several years, but at least we shouldn't be surprised when they do, since we have gone to the trouble to find out about them. And perhaps readers will also come to the conclusion that a little more knowledge about the European Community means a little less anxiety about the future. Some might even decide that, like the majority of people in Holland and in Luxembourg, they too could eventually become . . . happy Europeans.

1 Let's get this show on the road

A borderline case . . .

What is the point of a united Europe that's cut into pieces by borders? Not much, is the answer that comes to mind as we, the great travelling public of the Community, shuffle slowly through passport control at London, or Paris, or Frankfurt airport, surrounded by a more or less seething mass of other 'EC passport holders only' or as we stew away in our oven-hot cars under a sadistic sun, waiting for customs officers to relent and put an end to their strike at some Franco-Italian or Franco-Spanish border. As for having to open our suitcase and try to convince a stony-faced official that we are not in the habit of sniffing our own talcum-powder, while time runs out for that business meeting scheduled in the next half-hour . . . it's enough to make anyone wonder who on earth is benefiting from all this European unity, because it certainly doesn't look like it's going to be us – or is it?

Are European borders going to disappear as from 1 January 1993 and will we go back to the good old days of our forebears who used to trundle around the Continent on or behind their horses without giving a thought to such impedimenta as passports, identity cards or animal health certificates?

It is in fact one of the main results European leaders and officials have been striving towards in the last six to seven years, though whether they will have got there by the beginning of 1993 is a moot point. Obviously, the thunderous clap of thousands of checkpoint barriers crashing down all over the Community on the last stroke of twelve, 31 December 1992, would have a highly symbolic value and would certainly show the world that, in true Manchester spirit, when Europe says United, it means United. We must however face the fact that, even though European Community citizens will eventually be able to travel virtually unhindered throughout the EC, various forms of control will always exist and checkpoints will still be there at the borders.

But measures have been, and are still being, taken to reduce this notion of border control to a bare minimum – although some EC countries are going about it faster than others. The way things are for the moment, the United Kingdom looks as if it is going to be one of the last to relax controls. The main problem that needs to be solved is that of non-EC nationals: should inter-Community borders be maintained exclusively for them or not? The majority of Community countries consider that from the moment a non-EC traveller has arrived in an EC State and has therefore gone once through police and customs control, that traveller should be allowed to circulate freely within the Community, like any EC national. Britain would prefer to see freedom of circulation limited to EC nationals. The trouble is that EC citizens do not go around with their nationality stamped on their faces so they would have to stop at borders anyway, if only to prove their own identity and citizenship, just like they do now. The only difference would be that then they would be able to go straight through the Green customs channel, whatever they happen to be carrying with them . . .

Allowing individuals uncontrolled border access is proving to be a far more difficult question to settle than one concerning freedom of circulation for goods, services or indeed financial assets. That's because Community institutions are directly responsible for the latter problem and can therefore take the appropriate decisions relatively quickly and coherently, using, when a vote is necessary, the simple majority system whereas freedom of circulation for people is still a matter for each national jurisdiction, which explains why the United Kingdom can do one thing, France another, etc. The whole thing must therefore be sorted out by means of bilateral negotiations between individual States.

It also explains why certain EC member States have achieved a separate agreement and will open up their common borders earlier than the rest of Europe. They are the countries who signed the Schengen Convention of 1990 (see Chapter 9) – France, Germany, Belgium, the Netherlands, Luxembourg, Italy, Spain and Portugal.

But just because the European Commission and Parliament do not have the power of direct decision on the question, it doesn't mean they can't give their opinion and come up with suggestions and proposals that can then be examined by the European Council of Ministers. Various ad hoc committees have also been busy for many years, sorting out each particular problem according to their respective capabilities.

The question of freedom of travel for individuals does really need to be explained separately from that of freedom of movement for goods, services and capital, since things are not moving at the same speed for both.

WHAT PRICE UNTRAMMELLED TRAVEL?

1 Humans yes, bombs no . . .

1989 was the year when a great deal of work was done on the question of border controls for EC nationals, in particular during the Heads of State summits of Madrid in June and Strasbourg in December. The European leaders agreed on a basic text, known as the 'Palma Document', specifying the problems that needed to be solved before border controls could even start being abolished. The document identifies four main difficulties.

Terrorism

The fight against terrorist activities within and without the Community required a stronger and more efficient cooperation between police forces of the various member States. The ways and means of reinforcing this cooperation are being studied by the Ministers of the Interior and of Justice, working within a structure known as the 'Trevi Group'. This group has been meeting twice a year since 1976 to exchange information and coordinate national policies in the fight against terrorism and crime.

Drug smuggling

Here, cooperation was essential not only between police forces, but also between customs departments, as well as between police AND customs. As with terrorism, the aim was to install stronger and more efficient controls at all borders separating the EC from the outer world, and to speed up exchange of information. All work on this question is centralized and coordinated by a special European Anti-Drugs Committee set up by decision of the Strasbourg summit of December 1989.

Immigration

Who decides if and how an immigrant is allowed to reside in an EC country? The answer agreed upon by the Heads of State was to leave the decision to one specific member State – the one where the immigrant files his residence request. Once that decision is made, be it yea or nay, all the other States should abide by it. So, for instance, any non-EC national expelled by one EC country should not be able to re-enter the Community by going through another EC country.

This decision led to a first practical step being taken: in June 1990, the EC leaders signed a convention laying down the common rules to be observed by every State administration when examining a request for asylum. This convention was drafted, there again, by an ad hoc committee made up of the twelve Ministers in charge of immigration.

Data protection

Computerization of all sorts of information concerning private individuals is not governed by the same rules or even the same habits in all the EC countries. What is considered as perfectly normal information to be stored in a database system in one State is denounced in another as a blatant attack against the rights of the individual. The European Commission therefore spelt out a series of proposals aimed at guaranteeing the protection of people's private life.

Once these four main questions are sorted out, practical

measures can be taken to facilitate travelling between the various EC countries. Thse measures have already been worked out by the European Commission.

2 Sidling towards a duty-free Europe

When these measures are – eventually – adopted, travel for EC nationals within Community boundaries will hopefully be quicker and easier.

– Systematic customs control of luggage and objects carried by travellers will no longer be enforced – unless, of course, there is a security problem. Better inter-State cooperation should ensure that drug smugglers or illegal immigrants are identified and stopped systematically. In any case, ideally, smuggling drugs between, say, Amsterdam and London, should become as meaningless as 'smuggling' them between Buckinghamshire and Bedfordshire.

– Excise on goods like alcohol, tobacco, perfume, etc. is supposed to disappear by 1 January 1993. After that date, every European should, normally, be able to buy whatever consumer product he wishes wherever he wishes in the EC without having to pay further taxes at the border. In the meantime, the authorities are working up to it by increasing, as from 1 July 1991, the allowance of taxed goods for each traveller within the EC. It has gone up from 390 ECUs (£273) to 600 ECUs (£420) for consumer goods: the allowance for alcohol should be 12 bottles of spirits, 120 bottles of wine and 189 litres of beer as from 1 January 1993.

One of the problems being discussed is that of duty-free shops. Once duties are abolished, duty-free shops won't have much point inside the Community and will only be useful to travellers entering or leaving the EC. This, as you can imagine, will mean a hefty financial loss for airports and ferries, so a certain amount of lobbying went on, resulting in 'duty free' within the EC being maintained until 1999.

– Even though borders will still exist, we won't be needing so many customs officials at the 'inner' borders, i.e. the actual, physical separation between the EC countries.

Obviously, at airports, where flights leave for and arrive from all over the world, customs control will still be very much in force for those who come from outside the EC, but road or rail checks will decrease. This will mean fewer customs officials; in fact, there will be several thousand jobs destined to disappear, so, if one of your children is tempted by a career in Customs and Excise, it may be a better policy to steer them towards the police force, who will have a lot on their hands. The Drugs Squads, in particular, are going to be kept as busy, if not busier, until every EC country adopts the same policies on that difficult question. For instance, either everybody legalizes 'soft' drugs, or nobody does, but it won't be possible to go on having them considered as legal in certain EC countries like the Netherlands or Spain, and not in others, as is the case today. And, if borders are disappearing for potential criminals, how can they be maintained for the various national police forces? All these questions, and many similar ones, have yet to be sorted out before some sort of coherent border policy can really be achieved.

As for those customs officials who do keep their jobs, they are going to face an even tougher task as they man the remaining EC borders. Whatever their nationality and place of work, they are going to have to obey the same rules all over the Community. To start with they will have to come to terms with the fact that they will be working in the interests of the whole Community and not just their own country. This will mean a vast exchange of information, and of people, between the various European customs services. The European Commission has set up a programme called '**Matthaeus**', which caters for some 22,000 customs officials: they will be given the opportunity to go on exchange visits to EC countries other than their own, to go on training courses or to learn languages.

This programme is already under way and has involved several hundred people since 1990.

On top of that, the Community is working on a common customs legislation, so that the same regulations and the same spirit apply at every single Community border, from Greece to Denmark, and there is no weak link in the chain protecting Europe.

– At airports, a system will have to be worked out whereby passengers coming in from one EC country to another – or flying out from one to another – will be able to go through a special 'quick' channel. This would be the case for all passengers on inter-European flights, even those who are not EC nationals, since they would have already gone through 'normal' control on arrival at their first EC airport.

– Passports will continue to be issued by the authorities of each member State to their own citizens. However, as has been the case in most member States since 1985, all new passports will look the same: a maroon cover bearing the words 'European Community' above the name of the country of issue. Each State will also retain its own habits as far as period of validity, price, etc. are concerned. Nor will there be any change, apparently, for those countries who do not issue identity cards. British, Irish, Dutch and Danish nationals will therefore still need passports – as forms of identification – to travel within the Community; for the rest, an identity card will be sufficient, as it is now.

– Visas, like passports, will still be granted, for the time being, by each member State. The ultimate objective is, however, a common European visa. In the meantime, the various EC countries are, at the very least, going to try to adopt a common attitude, though it isn't easy.

Practically every European country has, for historical reasons, privileged relationships with some other part or parts of the world. Britain and the Commonwealth, Spain and South America, France and francophone Africa, etc. Once borders are opened, there is not going to be much point in one country refusing to grant a visa to a non-EC national if another one does.

The countries belonging to the Schengen group have already harmonized their policies on the question of visas. For instance, Italy, who did not demand entry visas for nationals from North Africa, will now do so because all the other Schengen countries demand one. On the other hand, Polish nationals no longer need visas to enter the countries of the Schengen group, thanks to a German initiative.

THE DELIGHTS OF TRANSPORT

1 Travelling by car

Crossing borders

Checkpoints at inter-European borders will still be in existence and they will be manned by police or customs officials, even though there may be less of them in view. Cars will not be stopped and passports checked as is usually the case at the moment (at least for the non-Schengen countries); travellers will be required to drive through at a slow pace, so that officials can stop them if necessary. At some borders, this is already being done and nobody will notice much difference; at others, like the British Channel ports, it could mean a noticeable gain of time for drivers who usually spend a quarter to half an hour being filtered through passport and customs control.

Another great tradition on its way out!

One idea under consideration is that vehicles transporting European Community nationals would carry a green sticker with a capital E on it: this would mean that all the occupants are EC nationals and that consequently they have nothing to declare.

The European Parliament has suggested that some form of visual control be extended to foot travellers, so as to avoid every one of them being stopped.

Safety

In February 1991, a group of experts completed a report requested by the European Commission on conditions of road safety in the Community and possible ways of improving it. The results of the report were hair-raising.

From 1957 to 1991, in the twelve member States, road casualties amounted to two million dead and forty million wounded. In one year, fifty thousand people on average are killed or wounded in road accidents throughout the Community. As for the cost, it is estimated at between 45 and 90 million ECUs (£31 million and £63 million).

The numbers vary considerably from one country to another. The safest place for driving is the Netherlands, with 92 road deaths per million inhabitants (= 236 per million cars), while the most dangerous is Portugal – 335 road deaths per million inhabitants (= 1,163 per million cars). A difference of one to four . . . Generally speaking, it is twice as dangerous to drive in Europe as it is in the United States.

According to the report, if all the other European countries followed the example of the more safety-conscious ones (which, incidentally, include Britain), it would be possible to save at least 25,000 human lives each year.

These conclusions prompted the Commission to outline a possible European Driving Code, to which the different member States could adhere on a voluntary basis, and not necessarily all at the same time. This is mainly because various countries are vigorously opposed to certain specific measures, for internal reasons, and accuse the Commission of exceeding its powers.

For instance, the Commission suggests limiting speed to between 100 and 130 km per hour (kph) on motorways and dual carriageways, and to between 80 and 100 kph in urban zones, with a 30 kph limit in town centres and residential districts. Germany, however, is totally opposed to speed restrictions on its motorways, and says it should all be left to the driver's 'sense of responsibility'. What a hope! Reducing speed is also a means of reducing the amount of carbon dioxide in the atmosphere – especially in Germany, where acid rain is killing off the forests.

Other suggestions put forward by the Commission are already being implemented in most EC countries, or will be shortly. Compulsory use of seat-belts in all the seats is already being enforced in a certain number of member States. The Commission would like to add another safety measure: transporting children would be forbidden in vehicles that do not have the necessary safety facilities (child locks; etc.).

Taking a lead from Sweden, the Commission also wishes to oblige drivers to keep their headlights on, dipped, by day as well as by night, and in all weathers, not only in rain or fog.

Finally, the Commission has asked that, from 1 January 1993, the alcohol level in the blood be limited to 0.5g per litre in every Community country. The experts' report officially confirmed what every careful driver is well aware of: drink is the main cause of road accidents, together with speeding. The problem will be to enforce the drinking and driving laws – after all, maximum alcohol level permitted is already 0.5g per litre in Portugal, but, as not many people seem to be obeying the law, the results are not very encouraging.

The vehicle

● A European MOT – or, more specifically, a set of common rules to be observed by all – should be in force by 1995 for all vehicles four years old or over registered in the EC. There again, the situation is very different according to each country, so the definitive MOT should be achieved in three stages.

– 1990-92: the control should cover 52 different points of the vehicle. However, repair should be compulsory for only 12, including brakes, lights and tyres.

– 1993-95: repairs would be compulsory on 26 points, including the body of the car.

– after 1995: all 52 points will be subject to compulsory repair when necessary.

● As from January 1992, tyres on all EC cars have to have grooves of a minimum 1.6 mm depth. Actually, this is compulsory for any vehicle, not only a car, carrying less than ten people, including lorries weighing up to 3.5 tons.

● As from 1 July 1992, all cars with an engine of a cubic capacity under 1.4 litres will have to be equipped with three-way catalytic converters. The aim is to reduce exhaust fumes by 50%. This will concern new models, of course. After January 1993, the measure will be extended to all new cars, whether large or small. Naturally, this will mean a spectacular boost in the use of lead-free petrol throughout Europe.

● Licence plates, eventually, will all have a standard shape and size. The European Commission suggests a 52 × 11 cm plate, with national numbers and letters etched out in black on a white or yellow background framed by a black border. On the left-hand side would figure the European flag and the letter identifying the country.

Documents

● There is, for the moment, no European driving licence although, since 1985, the same model (a pink tryptich) is now available throughout the Community. EC nationals residing in an EC country other than their own can keep their original licence for a year from the day they obtain their residence permit – then they must exchange it for a local licence. They will only get theirs back if and when they settle back home.

The European Commission has issued a directive stipulating that – rather than elaborating a common driving test – each member country recognize the validity of the tests held in all the other member States. This would then lead, in 1996, to a common driving licence based on the twelve national tests and issued for different lengths of time, according to the rules prevailing in each country.

The problem, of course, is that all the member States have to start by agreeing on a minimum amount of basic points so as to be sure that driving tests conform to certain standards.

The minimum age for obtaining a licence to drive cars or motorbikes will generally be eighteen, though in those countries where it is now seventeen that is how it will remain.

● Vehicle insurance for private individuals has, to a certain extent, been 'Europeanized' since 1973. Before then, owners of a car driven from one EC country to another had to obtain a green card proving they had the necessary insurance. This is not compulsory any more – except in Greece. A national insurance will protect the car and its occupants throughout the Community and, in case of accident or damages, the owner's insurance company will make the necessary arrangements – including negotiating with the insurance(s) of any other vehicle involved.

● After 1993, every EC citizen should be able to buy the car he wants in the EC country he chooses and have it registered back home. It'll be a question of getting the cars to correspond to a certain number of precise common standards and, as things stand, there are only two or three points, out of more than forty, that need to be agreed upon. For British and Irish citizens, however, this information is of limited interest, since there's not much point in them buying a car on the Continent, unless they particularly relish driving on the left in a car with a left-hand drive . . .

Talking of which, those same British and Irish drivers need not fear they will be forced to drive on the right-hand side of the road in their own countries. Don't think the question hasn't cropped up – it has, and it has been given a great deal of thought. However, even the most determined, the most fanatical supporters of a united Europe quailed at the thought of the effort and the danger involved. As for the expense of changing all the cars, the road signs, the traffic lights, etc., it would reach astronomical proportions! Especially if you add to all that the massive therapy treatments needed to cure two nations of traumatized drivers, passengers and policemen . . .

Roads

The Commission has requested a specialist report on the possibilities of a European motorway network to be completed by the year 2010. (The network, not the report, hopefully.)

The Commission would also like financial support to be given to three main types of road projects:

* a series of major link-ups between existing networks: the Brenner axis between Northern Italy and Europe; in the Pyrenees, the Toulouse–Barcelona link-up through the Puymorens Tunnel, to be operational by 1994; another one from Toulouse to Madrid; and one from Bordeaux to Valencia.

* reinforcing road communications with the more peripheral member States, namely: a direct Crewe to Holyhead road for a link-up with Ireland; an Athens–Patras road for a link-up with Brindisi in Italy; and a Madrid–Lisbon axis.

* improving connections with neighbouring non-EC countries by means of a motorway from Athens to Yugoslavia (if it still exists . . .); and, in Denmark, from Aalborg to the northern sea-port of Frederikshaven, for a link-up with Norway and Sweden.

2 Travelling by train

Border control

Rail passengers will probably benefit the most, in terms of convenience, from the suppression of inter-Community borders, provided they board a train leaving from an EC locality. The general idea is that they would not be submitted to any border control.

Another convenient measure that has at least the advantage of having been definitely adopted by the Council of (Transport) Ministers was taken in June 1991: member States' railway companies are now allowed to enter into joint ventures which allow them to offer services on one another's networks. This initiative is primarily aimed at freight transport in view, amongst other things, of the Channel Tunnel but, by facilitating inter-State railway management, it is in fact opening the door a bit wider on the suppression of national barriers. It is also an important step towards ending national railway monopolies, and bringing in competition between companies, which will give passengers a wider choice. It will also, eventually, mean the possibility for private capital to be involved and railway companies could then hope to get some return on the enormous structural investments needed to offer a modern network. That would also mean better trains and better service for passengers.

New networks

Improving the railway network is considered a top priority by the European Community leaders who fear that the whole EC territory is in danger of becoming one vast motorway filled with hordes of lorries. The Commission has therefore submitted a project providing for a vast high-speed rail system which includes 9,000 km of new railway lines and 1,200 km of link-ups between major lines.

It also outlines the need for a series of important links such as Paris–London–Brussels–Amsterdam–Köln to the north; Seville–Madrid–Barcelona–Lyon–Turin–Milan–Venice to the south, with spin-offs towards Lisbon and Oporto from Madrid, Tarvisio and Trieste from Venice.

Because of national differences in electrical systems, the European high-speed trains will have to be capable of functioning on three or four separate types of current. They will also have to negotiate different types of rail tracks and tunnel widths. For instance, when, after 1993, the TGV (Train à Grande Vitesse) will travel on the Paris–London line through the Channel Tunnel, special compartments will have to be built because, in Britain, trains are narrower, so an average-sized TGV would be too wide for a British tunnel.

3 Travelling by air

The two major preoccupations of European air travellers are, naturally enough, fares and security.

It is still an expensive business to travel by plane in Europe; it is, in fact, the most expensive in the world. So the European Commission has worked out a series of major projects, some of which are already being put into action.

Since 1988, national air companies who share a flight route – for instance London–Rome shared between Alitalia and British airlines, including British Airways – no longer do it on an automatic fifty-fifty basis. This means that the company who offers the best deal can obtain more flights than the others. By 1993, the best company should, theoretically, be able to get a particular connection all to itself, if it is very good. In practice, however, it would amount to giving a company a monopoly over a particular connection, which is exactly what everyone wishes to avoid, so competition will be maintained.

Another interesting measure should also be beneficial to travellers after 1993: if it wants to alter its fares, a company will no longer have to obtain permission from the governments of the countries connected by its flights (as is still the case); the assent of one country will be sufficient. In other words, if British Airways wishes to bring down its fares between, say, London and Amsterdam, it will only need permission from the British government (who, in this particular instance, may be more inclined to give it than the Dutch would . . .). On the other hand, if it is KLM who gets permission from the Dutch authorities to lower its fares to and from London, British companies may have no option but to follow suit if they don't want to suffer from the competition. The only way they could try to stop the Dutch would be to show that the KLM prices have dropped by more than 20% compared to the preceding year and that they are selling at a loss to attract passengers.

And what about companies from a third European country? Will Aer Lingus, for example, be allowed to run a regular flight between Paris and Athens? Not as such; however, what the company will be entitled to do is to stop in Paris on its way to and from Athens during its regular Shannon to Athens flight and pick up or drop off passengers (as many as will fill up to 50% of its plane seats).

Since April 1991, airline passengers can take advantage of the agreement reached by the Association of European Airlines (AEA) on the question of compensation for overbooking. Since that date, passengers on EC airlines who are refused admission on the plane where they booked a seat are entitled to compensation; they also get to choose between getting their fare back or being booked on another flight.

This greater (though not total) freedom of movement and fares may well lead to an increase in the number of flights over Europe. This will, of course, cause greater security headaches for the European authorities. There now exist 42 different centres and 22 different systems of air control throughout the Community. The Commission considers that this cannot be tolerated for much longer – such incoherence is just asking for trouble. The Commissioners would like to see all the air control centres functioning according to the same system and, eventually, using the same level of equipment. With this aim in mind, a central information unit is going to be set up in Brussels; it will gather information coming not only from the EC but from more than twenty European countries. This should make it a bit easier for European air traffic controllers to maintain secure (if not punctual) flights.

4 Travelling by ship

There is, unfortunately, not much to be said on that score, though one can always hope for the future. 1993 is not going to bring in any spectacular changes for ship passengers, or even for freight.

There is talk of a European merchant fleet, sailing under European colours, the EUROS flag, which may (according to a proposal made by the European Parliament) allow certain tax reductions. But there is not much being done about it for the moment, other than mutual recognition of national certificates of conformity. This is interesting for ship-owners, but bears no impact on the individual traveller.

However, it is important for that traveller to know that all measures applying to the control of motor vehicles at borders will also apply to pleasure-boats. In other words, the British owner of a British yacht or sailing-boat arriving in a French, Spanish or Italian port will not have to spend time on customs formalities. This will apply equally to river-boats.

5 Travelling with animals

1993 is not going to put an end to anti-rabies laws in the United Kingdom and Ireland. For the rest of the Community, domestic animals will be able to travel under the same conditions as their owners, i.e. without systematic border controls. Owners will, however, have to obtain a health and vaccination certificate, which they may have to produce at any moment on their travels.

6 Travel agencies

The European Commission has already taken certain measures to protect holidaymakers who use the services of travel agencies. This includes getting the profession to open a guarantee fund so that travellers can be reimbursed if a tour operator goes bust.

The Commission also forbids agencies to impose price supplements less than a month before departure date, even if they are justified by, say, a rise in petrol prices.

GETTING THE GOODS
VAN AROUND EUROPE

How a lorry-load of microwave ovens travels from Hamburg to Milan, or the adventures of a crate of oranges between Seville and Amsterdam is not exactly front-page material as far as the private individual is concerned and yet . . . Waitrose or Sainsbury's would definitely not be able to offer their usual wide choice of foreign delicacies if it weren't for a very efficient series of measures on freedom of circulation within the European Community.

As a matter of fact, if there is a field where the Single Market is really going to be effective, it is that of transport of goods and merchandise.

This is not very surprising, for a variety of reasons. Firstly, the suppression of obstacles to the free circulation of goods was, after all, the basic aim of the Founding Fathers of the Common Market, so a lot of work has been done on that over the years. Secondly, since 1971, customs duties are not levied by the various member states, but go directly into the EC budget (see Chapter 11). If nothing else, that was a particularly good reason for achieving a common policy as soon as possible.

Real progress was achieved, year after year, by steadily harmonizing customs procedures throughout the Community. This however did not mean that rules and regulations became any simpler; it just meant that they became more and more similar.

So, another important step forward was taken on 1 January 1988: until then, a driver carrying goods from one Community country to another, or through several Community countries, would need to fill in and present anything between seventy and one hundred and thirty different accompanying documents. After 1988, all that was needed was a Single Administrative Document, whether the goods were being carried between EC countries or being exported to or imported from an outside country. Even this single document is due to be eliminated on 1

January 1993 for exchanges of goods within the Community. It will still be necessary for exchanges with outside countries.

All that companies will have to worry about will be the strictly commercial documents and the ones concerning VAT. And even those are to become obsolete when all VAT systems are harmonized. Already, the average VAT rate has been fixed by the Twelve at a minimum of 15% (reduced rate is 5%). But VAT won't be really harmonized until about 1996, by which time everyone, hopefully, will have agreed on the principle that value added tax must not be paid in the country where the goods are bought or the services rendered, but in that of the client. So if, for instance, VAT on washing-machines is 18% in France and 17% in Britain, a company based in France will always pay 18% VAT on those appliances, even if it buys them in Britain. For the moment, the situation is exactly the contrary.

As private individuals, we may not feel immediately concerned by such measures, but as consumers we are bound to be involved as all these changes will automatically influence the price of consumer goods.

And, if removal lorries don't have to waste vast amounts of time at borders, those of us who are settling in another EC country may hope to get our furniture without too much delay. And less delay just might, with a bit of luck, mean less expense, especially as the Community has also granted haulage firms the right to transport goods for companies in EC countries other than their own. This means that a Spanish lorry delivering goods in Britain can work for a British company and take its goods to Spain instead of going back empty (which makes for an expensive trip, therefore expensive goods). The number of empty goods vehicles charging up and down EC motorways is not only a nuisance, but a danger to the environment.

STARS AND . . . STARS

There can't be many people in the world today who don't know what the European flag looks like. The ring of stars on a blue background has gained universal recognition. But how many people know how it came to look like that?

Pierre de Coubertin, the man who founded the modern Olympic Games, played an unwitting role in the business. When he designed the five rings of the Olympic flag, one for each continent, he coloured the ring of Europe in blue. So blue has remained as the colour of Europe and the symbol of the ring was also retained in the design of the twelve stars. As it happens, the fact that there are twelve stars and twelve member countries is a total coincidence. There have always been twelve stars and they will always remain so, even when other countries join the Community. The number twelve was chosen because, in heraldry, it represents perfection.

The flag was only adopted by the European Community in 1986. Before that, and since 1955, it was the flag of the Council of Europe.

2 Make yourself at home . . .

Whereas travelling from one EC country to another still involves a certain amount of security or customs checking and red tape, the process of taking up residence in a member State which is not one's own has been considerably simplified, to the extent that the European authorities have not thought it really necessary to bring in many new measures.

However, that right to reside in any EC country – for any EC national – is mainly linked to the right to work there. In other words, no Community country will happily allocate a residence permit to an unemployed person, although that person is a national of another member State (see page 26). Students and pensioners, as 'non-earners', are placed in another category and they do need to have their rights protected by special measures, which the Commission has elaborated (see page 21).

So, as things stand, we must assume that whoever is moving from his own EC country to another EC country is doing so because he has a job lined up, or else is going into some form of business or commercial activity there.

HOMING IN

Before getting anywhere, the first step is obviously to leave the place where you are currently staying. A European Council directive dated 15 October 1968 expressly demands that member States grant their own nationals the right to leave in order to establish themselves in another member State; this right is exercised by simply producing a valid identity card or passport at the point of exit. This right extends to the members of the family dependent for their support on the person who is leaving. Naturally, the State authorities also have the right to stop people leaving provided they have a valid reason, based on a problem of security, or health, or of public policy (for instance, it is generally public policy not to allow minors to waft out of the country without legal permission from the appropriate adults).

And, in case it had not made its meaning clear enough, the Council specifically stated that no exit visa or equivalent document should be demanded from EC nationals leaving their own country to go and live in another Community country.

Having thus, hopefully, established to everyone's satisfaction that an EC citizen is, in the normal course of events, allowed to leave his or her country without royal or presidential permission, the Community authorities went on to specify exactly in what circumstances the aforementioned citizen would be authorized to settle as a resident in another EC country. Entry, as we all know, is no more of a problem than exit. A valid passport or identity card is all that is needed. Even for the nationals of the countries belonging to the Schengen group, and who are crossing a land border between two Schengen countries, it is imperative to possess one of these two documents, although, in principle, they are not going to be submitted to any form of border control. They cannot run the risk of a random border check and the absence of any form of identification would be a very serious offence.

Having entered the country, it becomes necessary to obtain a residence permit, valid for five years and renewable. The 1968 Council directive specifies that the only documents required are the passport or identity papers displayed on arrival and a certificate of employment. A work permit is no longer necessary. If you are not a salaried employee but are self-employed, you will need to prove that you are earning enough for your upkeep and that of your family. That is usually done through the legal or banking organizations you are dealing with in the country of residence.

Normally (although this is not specified in the EC directive), you will also have to give proof of domicile. The reason it is not stated in the EC measures is that proof of domicile is required for everybody, including nationals of the country you are settling in, when establishing identity documents such as passports, driving licences, medical cards, etc.

The same measures apply to the members of your family, even if they are not EC nationals. They, however, will need an additional document, proving their relationship with you – a marriage or birth certificate, for instance. They will also have to produce a document issued by the competent authorities (town hall, for example) specifying that they were living with you in your native country. This is obviously no problem if it concerns a spouse or children, but it needs more careful consideration when it comes, for instance, to elderly parents who may not necessarily have been living under the same roof as you and who may wish to join you in your new country of residence. It all hinges on their financial status: according to whether or not they are financially dependent on you, the formalities will be different.

Your residence permit will remain valid even though you may have to leave the country, provided your absence does not exceed six months. It also stays valid in the case of young men who have to return to their native country for a period of military service, whatever the length of that period.

A residence permit must be issued free of charge or, in any case, must not cost you more than it would normally cost the nationals of the country to obtain an identity paper.

A temporary residence permit is also available for an EC national who has to go and work in another EC country for less than a year but more than three months. No residence permit is necessary for anyone whose stay in another EC country – for work or for leisure – does not exceed three months.

Progress has not been as steady or as simple when it comes to pensioners and students – or to that practically extinct category of people who do not have to earn their living because they have a 'private income'. Bertie Wooster, P. G. Wodehouse's immortal man about town, had he lived in the nineties and wished to settle on the Riviera would obviously have had more problems than Jeeves, his equally immortal gentleman's gentleman, who was a wage-earner. The operative word in that instance is 'Riviera'. The reason it took so much time for the Twelve to come to some agreement on 'non-active' residents was mainly that this category of the population had a tendency to gather in the same areas.

Countries like Spain and France were not all that keen to welcome hundreds of thousands of pensioners from all over the northern half of the Community – they did not, understandably, wish to see their coastal areas become so many European Floridas. What they were most worried about was the potential drain on their national health and pension services.

This also applied to students who, although they are 'non-earners', are entitled to benefit from the health services of the country where they reside and consequently represent an additional drain on public finances without being an economic asset. It would obviously have been rather unjust – especially with the growing numbers both of students and of pensioners in Europe – to expect two or three countries (and not always the richest, at that) to bear the financial brunt of catering for a non-active population.

It was important to sort out the problem without creating complicated administrative obligations and, most important, without impinging on people's basic right to live where they want. That, after all, is one of the fundamental principles of the European Community – for moral as well as economic reasons.

The solution worked out by the Commission and agreed on by the Twelve is the following:

– To obtain their residence permit, EC pensioners must simply prove that their pension exceeds the amount of aid normally given by the State where they are going to reside. In other words, that they have enough to live on without having to be allocated supplementary benefits from the authorities of their host country.

– As for students, their right of residence is obtained when they have completed their matriculation at whatever university attracts them and are covered by some form of medical insurance – State or private – either in their own country or their country of residence. They must also have sufficient income to cover their needs – in the normal course of events, students are not supposed to be on the dole. Should they, for some reason or another, find themselves in a position to receive certain State allocations (a student may have a child or children, for instance), these will be granted according to the system prevailing in the country of residence, but the money itself will be paid out by the authorities of the student's native country. It is therefore advisable to have some ideas of the social system in force in the country of residence; taking, once again, the question of parenthood, the French State does not grant family allowance in the case of an only child, whereas Britain does.

All this leaves unanswered the problem of the Bertie Woosters of Europe – they are still in limbo, poor souls, because, for complicated legal reasons, their case requires a unanimous agreement by the European Council, while right of residence for students and pensioners only needed a simple majority vote. This doesn't mean they aren't allowed to settle in whatever EC country they wish, but it is not, as for all other Europeans, an *automatic* right; it still depends on the goodwill of the authorities in the country where they wish to reside.

Finally – and this applies to all EC nationals, whatever their personal situation – anyone moving to another Community country is naturally entitled to bring their personal goods and chattels with them, and to benefit from special franchise, because of their EC nationality. There are no duties or VAT on their personal belongings, provided they have owned them for more than six months.

WORKING IT OUT

Another fundamental and inalienable right of the EC national is the right to work in the Community country of his choice. Which is all very well on paper: the question is whether this right can really be enjoyed in practice. Is it really possible for a Greek doctor, with Greek medical diplomas, to set up practice in the UK, for a Belgian barrister to defend a client before a Spanish court, for a German maths teacher to work in a French State school, etc.? That is really the fundamental problem.

However, before going into practicalities, there are a certain amount of basic principles that apply to one and all.

The principles

The European Council regulation dated 15 October 1968 specifically states that 'mobility of labour within the Community must be one of the means by which the worker is guaranteed the possibility of improving his living and working conditions, and promoting his social advancement, while helping to satisfy the requirements of the economies of the member States'. The regulation also specifies that 'all nationals of member States have the same priority as regards employment as is enjoyed by national workers'. Translated from Eurospeak, it means that any EC national can go and work in any EC country he or she wishes, if it's going to make him live better and benefit the economy of the host country, and there should be no discrimination against him. There are exceptions, however, when it comes to public service – the army, diplomacy, the judiciary, the police are reserved for the nationals of each EC State.

A Council directive (and not regulation) of 15 October 1968 also specifies that anyone having signed a work contract in another EC country does not have to wait for residence formalities to be completed before starting work in that country, on the date stated in that contract.

The directive also states that a valid residence permit may not be withdrawn from an individual on the grounds that he is no longer employed in the country of residence – either temporarily for reasons of health or because his employers have sacked him. The same rights apply to people who live in one member State and go to work in another, provided they go home at least once a week (this is a frequent occurrence, for instance, between France and Germany), to people who are going to do a job in another EC country for less than three months (say a British builder working on a holiday home on the Continent) and to seasonal workers possessing the relevant contract of employment issued in the country of residence (a farm worker employed to pick fruit . . .).

These rights were granted to self-employed workers in May 1973, by means of a Council directive specifying that 'each member State shall grant the right of permanent residence to nationals who establish themselves within its territory in order to pursue activities as self-employed persons'. It does, however, go on to indicate 'when restrictions on these activities have been abolished'. These restrictions must apply to everybody, including the nationals of the State of residence; if they are not allowed to pursue certain activities because in that country they are considered illegal or are subject to some form of public monopoly (printing bank notes or official documents, for example) then other EC nationals will be subject to the same restrictions. When it comes to allowing foreign EC nationals to take up jobs, a country, without actually forbidding them access to certain professions, can extend certain rights exclusively to its own nationals. This is the case, in particular, when it comes to the legal professions. In several countries, for instance, a notary is not only an independent professional, but also a public officer appointed and controlled by the Ministry of Justice. As such, the notary is entitled to authenticate signatures on a document – thereafter these signatures cannot be challenged in the eyes of the law. A member State is allowed to limit this power to notaries who are its own nationals.

Having said all that, there are rights which extend to all workers within the European Community, be they salaried employees or self-employed professionals.

– Working conditions must be the same for a non-national as for a national. This includes salaries, working hours, promotion, leave of absence (for military service, maternity, etc.), dismissal, pensions, etc.

– Living conditions must be the same. This concerns access to housing, medical services, family benefits, fiscal advantages, transport facilities, etc.

– Access to vocational training or adult education facilities must be identical; this also applies to schooling for the children of EC nationals.

– Union rights must also be observed. A worker from another EC State, says the European Council, 'shall enjoy equality of treatment as regards membership of trade unions and the exercise of the rights attached to this membership, including the right to vote and to be eligible for the administration and management posts of a trade union'. However, the European Community has made no provision authorizing closed shop practices. In fact, Britain is the only Community country where such practices are still relatively widespread. In France, they are limited to printers and dockers. But, all it needs is for a worker coming from another EC country to appeal to the European Court of Justice on the grounds of discrimination; if his appeal is successful, it would create a precedent that would be a very effective means of putting an end to closed shop tactics.

What happens later, to a worker who has reached retirement age? The Community also provides for this contingency.

An EC national who has resided at least three years and worked for at least the last twelve months of those years in an EC country other than his own is entitled to remain permanently in that country. This right is granted to all workers, in employment or self-employed. If a resident dies during his working life, whatever his professional activity, provided he had official right to reside in the host country, the authorities of that country will recognize the right of his family to remain on condition that:

a) the deceased had resided continuously within its boundaries for at least two years;

b) dies as a result of an accident at work or an occupational illness; or

c) the surviving spouse is a national of the State of residence (or even used to be one before getting married).

Finally, unemployed people. The EC authorizes an unemployed person to travel to a Community country other than his own and to reside there for up to three months if he is seeking employment in that country – sometimes longer if he can prove that he has a real chance of getting a job. During this period, he may continue to draw national insurance benefits in his own country, but not means-tested benefits (income support or family credit). Apart from this specific case, unemployment benefits cannot be exported. Normally, an unemployed person must register as such within a week of his arrival in the other country; he will then have to observe the rules of that country (signing on, etc.).

All these details and more are explained in a leaflet entitled UBL22, obtained from the Unemployment Benefit Office.

When it comes to finding a job, apart from the usual channels (newspapers, ads, contacts, etc.) there is an EC service, SEDAC, which keeps up-to-date information on vacancies throughout the Community. It is available through all Job Centres.

The reality

The principles of the right to work having been well and truly established, the reality of the situation was not quite so simple. A certain number of very precise obstacles remained.

The question of 'public service' professions had to be sorted out, so that the same meaning would be given to the expression all over the Community. One can understand the authorities of a nation preferring to employ one of their own when it comes to policemen, soldiers, diplomats or magistrates, but is it really necessary to extend this preference to school teachers, nurses, postmen, train drivers or TV cameramen? What harm could befall the security of a member State if these professions were opened to other Europeans? And yet these were some of the professions which, in various EC countries, depended on the State or on public companies, and therefore came under the heading of Civil Service. This could bring about some ridiculous situations: France, for instance, who does not have enough maths teachers, could not use the services of teachers from Germany (who has too many) in its State schools, where teachers hold the status of civil servants.

After years of pushing and prodding obstinate State authorities, the European Commission is at last getting somewhere. Even the most adamant countries, such as France and Germany, have accepted the principle suggested by the Commission, based on sound common sense. Certain 'sensitive' professions, where the interests of the State are directly involved, will remain partly or totally closed to foreigners – the army, the police, the diplomatic service, central banks (such as the Bank of England, or the Bundesbank), inland revenue, as well as local or county government services. All other professions must, as from January 1993, be open to nationals from all over the European Community. This means mobility – if they so wish – for millions of people.

Still, considering the time and trouble it is taking to set up this cross-fertilization, one wonders how our various sovereigns of centuries past would have coped if they had restricted their armies to their own subjects, instead of relying heavily on mercenary regiments from all over Europe. Even the American and French armies who were allies in the American War of Independence were partly made up of German soldiers – to the extent that, what with one thing and another, German just missed, by a hairsbreadth, becoming the national language of the United States. Which conjures up interesting hypotheses on the possible outcome of the two World Wars . . .

Another very practical problem is that of equivalence of diplomas and competence. This immediately fires the imagination with nightmare visions of tragedies created by lack of competence in doctors, dentists, midwives, chemists, in short any profession dealing with people's health. But in any profession, it is vital for an employer to be sure that he can use the right sort of person for the right sort of job, all over Europe if necessary. Considering the enormous amount of different professions, the authorities of the European Community have taken several types of measures, covering vast chunks of the professional world.

a) They put in the same bag all professions that required a minimum of three years' university education. Since January 1991, university degrees obtained after these minimal three years are recognized throughout the EC. This involves such professions as lawyers, engineers, secondary or primary school teachers. It is called the 'First General System of Mutual Recognition of Qualifications'.

b) They made out specific directives for the professions that are subject to a different and particular legislation in each country. This concerns, for instance, doctors, veterinarians and transport operatives. This, however, was before 1985. Since then, a single general directive has been worked out and any profession subjected to special legal regulations is now covered by that single directive.

c) Finally, there remained the problem of all the other professions, the ones which require less than three years' university education. They were all divided into nineteen different professional categories. Within these categories, there are vast numbers of different professions and professional levels. It was decided to start from the bottom rung – qualified operatives – and climb the ladder until the three-year university level was reached. By June 1990, only five out of the nineteen categories had been officially sorted out: catering and hotel management; car repairs; building; electricity and electronics; agriculture-horticulture-sylviculture. This may, on the face of it, not seem much, but these measures of equivalence actually cover 137 different types of jobs. By 1993, all the other professional categories should have received their respective equivalences of diplomas and qualifications: in 1991 textiles industry, clothes and fashion, metal industry, office administration, chemistry, industry and research, trade, tourism, transport, food industry, and public works; in 1992 printing, woodwork, steel and iron industries, leatherwork.

There may, however, be delays, because it is a very long and drawn-out procedure. It is not simply a question of setting out equivalent diplomas. There are also such things as talent and competence that can be recognized in different ways according to different countries. So, every time, a specific job description has to be drawn up with groups of specialists from every country, each group including a spokesman for the workers, one for the employers and one for the State, with the help of the European vocational training organization CEDEFOP (Centre Européen pour la Développement de la Formation Professionelle), based in Berlin. Once a general agreement has been reached, then each member State has a period of seventy-five days in which to study it, to make sure there is no conflict with national or local rules that no one knew about.

Having sorted out the problem of equivalence for professional degrees and diplomas has been a great help when studying the final and essential problem: equivalent training. A diploma which in some countries is recognized immediately, will in others need to be completed by a period of practical experience or training. This is the case for architects. In other professions, a diploma can be replaced by proof of professional experience. A hairdresser or caterer, for instance, can work in an EC country other than his own if he can prove that he has worked for six consecutive years in a self-employed capacity or as manager of a hairdressing salon or restaurant, or else three consecutive years in one of those two capacities, plus five years minimum as an employee. He can then claim a 'European Community Certificate of Experience' which will be his professional passport to settling in another EC country.

In all cases of professional equivalence, specific information must be obtained for each branch. The people to contact are the relevant professional orders and organizations in each country. In the United Kingdom, the Department of Trade and Industry can also be most helpful. Finally, on a European level, CEDEFOP issues a useful guide to vocational training systems in all Community countries.

And, of course, whatever your diplomas, qualifications or experience, there is one vital point when it comes to working in another European country: the language. Jobs where some knowledge of the local language is not needed can be counted on the fingers of one hand – even though there is no law, national or European, allowing potential employers to reject a candidate on the grounds of language. However, they would be mad if they didn't take the problem into account – and so would any potential candidate for a job in another European country!

THE EUROPEAN STUDENT BODY GROWS MORE AND MORE FEMININE

In 1986-87, there were in the European Community 59,357,000 school children and students.

The number of primary school children has been regularly decreasing, due to the general lowering of the birth rate.

There were 29,093,000 in 1970; by 1987, there were 22,733,000.

The number of students, on the other hand, has gone on growing: 3,510,000 in 1970, 6,629,000 in 1987.

The main reason has been the growing number of girls who now continue their studies at university level: 46% of students in the EC are women.

3 Learning the lesson
(youth and education)

In an ideal and logical world, the chapter on education in the Community would have preceded the one on working there – but plain facts and common sense gave precedence to the immediate needs of Europe's working adults before getting down to preparing the future of its young.

It is however indisputable that the Community's best chance of existing and surviving as a single entity is through its young people and their awareness of the task that awaits them as well as the unprecedented opportunities that are offered them.

Jean Monnet, known as one of the Founding Fathers of the Community (see Chapter 8), once said that, given the chance to relaunch the EC, he would have started with education instead of the economy. It would certainly have been more difficult than catering to people's immediate economic and trade interests (and that's been difficult enough!) but it would most probably have given European unity an even more solid foundation.

The European Community is reaching a stage where it is obvious that economic interests alone will never be a sufficiently strong adhesive and that Europeans will stick together if they also share a sense of identity, of belonging to the same group. This can only be done properly through education. The young Britons of today who are in their late teens were born in a country that was already part of the European Community. It seems very difficult, if not practically impossible, to imagine for them a working life from which the European influence would be excluded.

Giving people the right to move and work freely within the Community is an important step, but these people also have the right to expect from the European authorities an educational platform that will facilitate and enrich this freedom of movement and exchange for their children. It is not a question of interfering with national school programmes and curricula, because that would be an attack on national identity, but the idea is to add a European dimension to those programmes by encouraging existing exchanges, sometimes through financial aid, and by offering practical opportunities of intra-Community travel, study and work to all young people (and not only to students).

Taking things step by step, and, in a sense, backwards, the Community went from examining the problems of adults to working on the question of young people – as opposed to children. Not only because they represent the more immediate future and must therefore be prepared as soon as possible to confront the professional challenge of the Single Market, but because the smaller children must start by shaping their knowledge and personalities through their own national education systems, thus receiving the good, solid grounding which prepares them for the wider horizons of a European experience.

That is not to say, however, that the Community authorities never gave a thought to the fate of younger children.

PRESCHOOL AND SCHOOL CHILDREN

The European Commission has gone very thoroughly, for instance, into the question of care for preschool children. The existing situations and the methods in use in all European countries, within or without the Community, were examined: the unanimous conclusion was that nowhere – with the possible exception of Sweden – are there enough facilities for the care of small children, whether at home or in day centres. As more and more women are going out to work, the result is a dramatic slump in the birth rate throughout Europe – with the exception of Sweden, where a systematic policy of developing infant and child care has led to the birth rate going up again.

For the moment, neither the Commission nor the European Parliament have gone further than carefully studying and comparing the various situations, and underlining the general need to improve and develop child care facilities for working families, or else the demographic trend will continue to point downwards and Europe will be well on the way to becoming, literally, an 'old' Continent.

That doesn't mean, however, that the Community authorities are going to sit on the fence for ever; there is every chance that the next generation of European parents will benefit from some form of Community policy governing the question of child care facilities.

Exchange schemes for European children, either individually or through their schools, are nothing new, and the Community sees no reason to do much except applaud and encourage them wholeheartedly. As a matter of fact, the Community isn't averse to gently pushing things a bit further by suggesting a more systematic and far-reaching exchange: a whole class would change places with an equivalent class from a school in another EC country, not for a few days, but for a whole month. Naturally, that month spent 'discovering' a different educational system – and getting to grips with another language – would be an active part of the year's school curriculum. There is still a lot of work to be done – on a European as well as a national level – before that sort of initiative can actually be put into effect throughout the twelve countries. It implies a lot of goodwill and organizational skill on the part of the various educational authorities – not to mention finding the necessary funds (although a Community project of this kind would certainly obtain a certain amount of funding from various European sources, and probably national ones as well).

In the meantime, freedom of circulation and the right to work in the Community means that more foreign teachers can be present in schools. In the UK, where teachers are not civil servants, generations of pupils were taught foreign languages by generations of Mesdemoiselles and Fräuleins. In the meantime, generations of French or German pupils were also taught a foreign language by generations of Mesdemoiselles (in France) or Fräuleins (in Germany), whether that language was English, Spanish or Russian. In most of the twelve EC countries, teachers, at least in State schools, are civil servants, which meant, until a short while ago, that only nationals of each country were allowed access to the profession. This is now changing (see page 27) and, in the years to come, children will not only learn to speak a foreign language – they might even get to pronounce it properly!

Furthermore, if exchanging whole classrooms of children needs careful financial consideration, it is possible, and certainly less expensive, to exchange individual teachers for a determined length of time, whatever their given subject matter.

This is actually being done already. Since 1989, some 1,600 secondary school teachers in the EC have benefited from the 'teachers' exchange' grant, aimed specifically at those who do NOT teach languages. Every year, some 400 teachers spend a month in a secondary school of another EC country, then welcome their 'co-respondent' to their own school for a similar period. They do not teach during their stay: the idea is for them to discover teaching methods and habits in their own subject, but in another country. Most of the time, this exchange is followed by other visits and contacts, with a view to building up a common project involving teachers and pupils from both sides.

Teachers who are interested must apply through the headmaster of their school. Usually, the school already has some form of exchange or cooperation scheme going with another European school, and the teacher's candidature will become part of that programme. After their stay abroad, teachers must submit a report. The grant covers transport and maintenance costs. This exchange programme is usually organized on a national level by the Ministry for Education. The Youth Exchange Centre can also be contacted.

A further step, in the foreseeable future, will be the opening up of school teaching posts to candidates from all over the Community. This is already done in Luxembourg, and there is no reason why it shouldn't happen elsewhere in the fullness of time. It would certainly be a very interesting professional experience for teachers and would help broaden children's minds from an early age.

OUT OF SCHOOL EXCHANGES

What the European Community already does is promote out of school exchanges for young people.

The European Social Fund, set up to finance all sorts of social policies in the Community, actually spends three-quarters of its annual budget on schemes, grants and scholarships aimed at helping young people between sixteen and twenty-five to become active members of the Community through education, training and exchange programmes. Some of these programmes are aimed at students, others at school-leavers who are doing vocational training, others still at youngsters who are starting their first job.

The Youth Exchange Programme, however, is aimed at all young people between the ages of fifteen and twenty-five, whatever their occupation. It promotes short cultural exchanges between groups belonging to different EC countries. These groups can be part of an already existing organization (youth clubs, Scouts, etc.) or they can be 'purpose-built' by young people who want to start an exchange programme. In both cases, EC funds can be provided. Obviously, the first thing to do is find a group with similar interests in another EC country (from ballet to bird-watching) – this is where organizations like twinning associations can come in very useful. The next step is to set up an exchange programme, keeping in mind that it has to have a distinct European flavour, and that it must not have any connection with school activities, sport, or politics. So, exchanges between rugby teams or Young Conservatives clubs cannot hope to get funding from the Youth Exchange Programme.

Finally, visits between groups, both ways, have to be organized within a period of two years, for two to three weeks. EC funds will cover half the cost of travel and board; the rest must be raised by the groups themselves through whatever fund-raising schemes they see fit to organize. To obtain EC funds, exchange programmes must be submitted to a regional committee, who will accept or reject them. The Youth Exchange Programme (some 80,000 exchanges were organized between 1989 and 1991) is particularly interesting for young people who would not normally benefit from the traditional exchange systems through families, sports clubs, schools, etc., perhaps because of their personal situation. It is also aimed at encouraging young people to use their initiative and organize their own projects.

STUDENTS

The perspective of the Single Market has given added impetus to the drive towards better knowledge and sharing of experience at university level. Since 1987, three major programmes have been launched, involving a steadily growing number of students throughout the Community.

– **Erasmus** was the first to be set up. Its aim is to help all higher education institutions who wish to give their students and teachers the opportunity to pursue their activities in another EC country for a stated amount of time. Erasmus covers every field of teaching and study – although there is a similar programme called 'Science' which is more particularly devoted to exchanges in scientific research.

Erasmus got off to a slower start than hoped for, but it has now picked up speed and is doing well: in 1991, some 40,000 European students benefited from its financial aid, which is practically as many in that one year as there were in the three preceding ones. This, it must be said, is mainly due to the fact that the European Council of Ministers doubled the Erasmus budget for 1990–94, with the idea that, by 1993, some 10% of European students should have acquired this 'cross country' experience. As with the other programmes, Erasmus does not grant funds to an individual, but to a teaching institution, such as a university or a college, for a particular course. Therefore, the starting point of the whole operation is to find out if the course a student is going to follow in his own country has the Erasmus seal of approval; this must be given not only by Brussels, but by the national Erasmus office.

This course may require a compulsory or optional period of study in another EC country. If it is backed by Erasmus, that will enable students to obtain a mobility grant. When the period abroad is optional, students do not, in the normal course of events, get anything over and above their usual maintenance grant – so Erasmus comes in very useful for covering travel expenses and the extra cost of living abroad. Students who can take advantage of the optional study period abroad actually get priority in the Erasmus programme over those whose trip is compulsory because, in the latter case, local authority grants tend to cater for the cost of maintenance and travel to another country. However, Erasmus funding can still be available to them to help face the higher cost of living. In all cases, students on the Erasmus programme are exempted from registration and tuition fees while studying abroad.

Anyone interested in benefiting eventually from an Erasmus programme would be wasting their time if they went directly to the Erasmus office in their own country. As already stated, the role of the national Erasmus office is to provide grants in chunks to the various higher education institutions, not to individuals. It is up to those institutions to decide on each individual case. So the people to go and see are those who are running the courses. Students who are interested in the Erasmus programme should start by finding out whether their future courses are backed by it and choosing those that are. And don't forget that Erasmus covers every type of course, whatever the chosen field of study. As for deciding the country to study in under the Erasmus programme, those who don't have a definite idea (and, more important still, a definite knowledge) of this other country's higher education system can consult an extremely detailed and useful handbook published by the Commission of the European Communities. It is called *Higher Education in the European Community* and provides all the necessary information, country by country, on the structure, the institutions, the requirements, the grants, the regulations of the higher education systems, as well as all the social aspects (health, accommodation, advisory services, etc.).

– The other programme born in 1987 was **Comett** – it also met with a lot of success. Comett sponsors links between businesses and universities or colleges with advanced technology courses (telecommunications, satellite, computer or information technology, etc.). It isn't limited to the EC but includes the EFTA countries – Austria, Finland, Iceland, Norway and Switzerland.

In 1990, Comett funded 876 projects (out of the 2,335 submitted) which represented more than double the 1989 figures. At the same time, the number of university–business partnerships placed under the aegis of Comett rose from 125 to 158.

These links between university and business take the form of University Enterprise Training Partnership (UETP). Both undergraduate and graduate students can spend a determined amount of time inside a company in another EC country for a practical instruction period partly financed by Comett. Obversely, young people already working in a firm that is a member of the UETP programme can be sent either to study or to gain practical experience in another EC country, always with Comett's financial backing.

There again, there is no individual funding. It is a question of finding out which college is directly involved in the UETP scheme, and on what subjects. (For the appropriate information, see address at end of book.)

One of the Community's major preoccupations is to multiply the links between education and vocational training on the one hand, scientific and technological development on the other. Which is why the Comett programme is complemented by a series of other, more specialized schemes, such as **Eurotecnet** (European Technology Network), whose aim is to stimulate exchanges and research on new technology in the field of vocational training and adult education. The idea is to determine areas that are, or will be, most in need of properly qualified personnel and to attract towards these areas – through appropriate training funds –people whose jobs are currently being put at risk by technological changes, especially in the small and medium-sized companies.

Another Comett-linked programme is **Delta**, whose aim is to help create and develop computerized equipment destined for teachers.

– In 1990, a third major programme was launched: **Lingua**, aimed at encouraging young people to learn another Community language. It finances grants, exchanges and teaching equipment, to help in the training of foreign language teachers. It provides funding for degree level courses which include at least a 50% language element. However, it also funds exchanges between EC nationals whose studies or vocational courses are below degree level (which neither Erasmus nor Comett do). So, if somebody is training to be a caterer, a hairdresser or a nurse, or is studying for B-Tech, 1st Diploma or B-National qualification, they can be candidates for a Lingua grant. Provided, once again, that their educational establishment applies for one, because it cannot be obtained individually. So, there again, those who are interested in learning another European language on top of their professional training need to find out which establishments benefit from the Lingua grant.

SCHOOL-LEAVERS
AND YOUNG WORKERS

– The best-known of the European programmes for the promotion of vocational training is **PETRA** (Preparation for Adult Working Life or 'Programme Européen pour le Travail des Adultes').

It will add extra funds to national projects already providing vocational training for young people aged sixteen to twenty-five, so as to give those projects a European angle and dimension. The money is used to establish links with similar schemes in other EC countries. PETRA will also back projects presented by young people so as to encourage initiative and creativity. It also funds research on economic, social and technological developments aimed at improving the quality of vocational training.

Before entering a vocational training scheme, those interested in this 'European dimension' should find out if the scheme already has an involvement with PETRA.

– For young people who have already started working but would be interested in widening their professional horizon, the Young Workers Exchange Programme offers a good opportunity. Candidates have to be aged eighteen or over and have work experience, or else a B-tech, a City & Guilds or have completed a youth training scheme.

YWEP backs organized links with other member States which allow employers to send young workers on an exchange visit to gain broader experience in the particular trade or industry they are working or training in. This means that young people from another EC country will also be coming to work or train in the UK on an exchange basis.

The aim of this programme is to give young people a working knowledge and an experience of life in another EC country; this can become an asset on the employment market. They should check with their employer or the people they are training with (their firm, further education college or local council) whether these already take part in the scheme. If they don't, it is possible, in this instance, to be an individual candidate, either by applying directly or by asking to be nominated by an employer for longer-term projects run by the YWEP itself. Individual projects could last three to four months.

When a project is accepted, a grant is issued to cover the cost of accommodation, travel, food, cultural activities and pocket money. Participants in longer-term projects receive a weekly payment.

OTHER PROGRAMMES

– For those who want to know more about teaching methods in the various member States and Community initiatives in the field of education, there exists a European database system called **Eurydice**. On top of which, the **Arion** programme gives financial backing to study and research trips aimed at helping those responsible for education increase their knowledge and understanding of the various national systems. The European Commission also organizes seminars and conferences involving the different categories directly interested in education policies: parents, teachers, employers, trade unionists.

– The purpose of the **Iris** network is to stimulate and support vocational training programmes designed to meet the needs of women. Funds are provided for exchange visits between groups participating in the network, seminars, and other ways of promoting information.

So, a lot is being achieved; but there is still a great deal of work to be done in favour of a more concerted and coherent approach of educational systems, without impinging on each country's autonomy. Even though everyone claims to be convinced of the importance of a European dimension in education, this dimension is still hardly ever taken into account when an education reform is launched in a Community country – nobody pays much attention to the possible repercussions on a European level, nor do they bother to examine other countries' experiences, which can sometimes be quite illuminating and might avoid certain mistakes being made twice. This is why the European Commission is relentlessly pursuing its efforts to strengthen the already existing cooperation and exchange network. It publishes many brochures and documents presenting comparative analyses of the various sytems; it continues consulting the member States on their preoccupations and their perspectives to see which points can be studied together; and, with this aim in mind, it encourages exchanges and discussions between the higher echelons of national administrations. Finally, the Commission wants to promote the creation of teams of 'transnational' experts whose European knowledge and experience would come in useful to the education authorities of each country when planning changes and reforms.

SCHOLARSHIPS AND AWARDS

A number of smaller funding systems are aimed at encouraging the study of European integration in universities.

– Robert Schuman Scholarships. The European Parliament offers scholarships to postgraduate students and young researchers for a one- to three-month period of work carried out in the Parliament.

– Jean Monnet Fellowships. Each year, the European University Institute offers thirty Jean Monnet fellowships to academics who wish to undertake full-time research in Florence on topics which contribute to the work of the University.

– Jean Monnet Project. To encourage universities to adapt certain courses, in particular law, economics, history, political and social sciences, so as to include Community developments and support research on European integration, funding is available to co-finance the opening of new three-year teaching posts; application forms can be obtained from University Information at the European Commission.

– Paul Finet Foundation. This Foundation provides support for the schooling and training of the children of coal miners and steel workers killed by an industrial accident or by an occupational disease.

– 'Stagiaires'. The European Commission provides the opportunity for a limited number of graduates to follow training courses of about five months at the Commission headquarters. Trainees or 'stagiaires' are recruited twice a year. Apparently, there are many candidates and competition is fierce, so applicants should seek information and advice well in advance from the UK offices of the Commission.

WHAT PRICE A CAR
IN EUROPE?

In 1991, the Nord-Pas de Calais regional consumer centre made a comparative study of car prices in seven EC countries, with interesting results.

For a large car (e.g. Renault 21 GTS), the price in round figures was:
- Belgium: £8,540
- Spain: £10,800
- France: £9,050
- UK: £10,230
- Luxembourg: £8,540
- The Netherlands: £8,270
- Germany: £9,930

The price of a medium-sized car (e.g. Ford Orion 1400 CLX):
- Belgium: £7,380
- Spain: (not sold there)
- France: £7,580
- UK: £9,850
- Luxembourg: £7,370
- The Netherlands: (not sold there)
- Germany: £8,260

The price of a small car (Peugeot 205 XL):
- Belgium: £5,320
- Spain: £5,920
- France: £5,680
- UK: £7,400
- Luxembourg: £5,360
- The Netherlands: £5,135
- Germany: £6,080

4 Europe's golden opportunity

When it comes to pounds and pence, the road leading to the Single Market seems to have been straighter and slightly less bumpy than in other Community transactions. But then, financial exchanges have always had a way of ignoring borders that most human beings would envy . . .

There is still a great deal that needs to be achieved, however, and in 1993 we will be miles away from the financial unity which would enable Europe to catch up with the big leaguers like the USA and Japan; nevertheless, since the European Community took on a new lease of life with the Single Act, both the Americans and the Japanese have stopped dismissing Western Europe as a jumble of economic nonentities and have been noticeably placing as many pawns as they could afford in European businesses, so as not to be caught napping after 1993.

All this financial acceleration is not just for the benefit of big business – or even little ones. It also affects the individual European, who buys property, opens bank accounts, invests in whatever he thinks best, takes out all sorts of insurance and, last but not least, pays tax, directly and indirectly.

MONEY MATTERS

Banks

1 July 1990 was just an ordinary day for all those millions of Europeans who did not happen to be celebrating their birthday or their wedding anniversary, but for the financial pundits of the Community, it was a milestone on the road towards the Single Market. It was the day when all movements of capital inside the Community were made definitely free. This meant that all remaining exchange controls were abolished, thus giving individuals as well as businesses total freedom to open bank accounts in any member State – there were no more controls on any account, current or deposit, on loans and on investment in short-term securities.

Although this new freedom affected, in principle, all EC countries, a transition period was extended to a few: Greece, Ireland, Spain and Portugal were given until 1992 to sort themselves out. So, by January 1993, a native of Barcelona will have no problem in opening a bank account in Birmingham, and an Irishman will be entitled to ask for a loan from a bank in Lisbon to set up a factory in his own country.

Another important Community directive, adopted in December 1989, will give European banks a second major breakthrough: as from 1993, they will be able to open agencies in whatever EC country they wish, without having to obtain preliminary authorization from that country's government. On top of that, these agencies will be controlled by their country of origin, not the one they are established in.

And that's not all: a bank will be allowed to offer its services in another EC country without even having to open an agency there. A British bank will be allowed to offer loans, for instance, to businesses or individuals in Italy without having opened a branch there; if, however, it wants to open one in, say, Rome or Milan, this branch will be answerable to the British financial authorities, not the Italian ones.

This freedom is not limited to banks – it is extended to all credit companies, including building societies, unit trusts, pension funds, etc.

For the individual consumer this, of course, means greater freedom to shop around, to pick and choose. Those countries whose financial institutions have more to offer are, naturally, going to benefit from this state of affairs, at least in the short term, until the others catch up. It also simplifies matters for these institutions in a most spectacular manner, since they have to worry about only one set of regulations, that of their own country, instead of twelve different ones.

All this implies a certain amount of mutual trust between member States, but the European Community authorities were well aware that one cannot let vast amounts of money go zig-zagging across the Continent on the basis of trust alone. Liberating movements of capital is one thing, sitting back and letting the law of the jungle take over is another, and not really typical of EC institutions. So a number of basic rules have been set out – the minimum required from any financial establishment that wishes to do business in the Community countries. This includes such things as minimum starting capital (normally five million ECUs), guarantees of honorability for the shareholders and auditors, information on the existing and future business structures of the institution, its involvement in activities other than financial, etc.

If a financial institution meets these EC requirements, the host country cannot stop it from operating on its territory even though its own banks or credit services may be hampered by more stringent rules. This does not mean, however, that the host country is powerless. It is naturally master of its own monetary and fiscal policy, which all financial institutions have to take into account.

The cost of credit, for instance, remains the prerogative of the national authorities. In other words, an organization – bank, insurance company, building society – cannot go around offering tax-free loans or policies in an EC country where these operations normally have some form of tax attached to them.

For the consumer, this wider choice should be accompanied by less expense. The European Commission has worked out that a more coherent and integrated financial system would normally cause banking costs to go down by some 10%. It will be interesting, for instance, to see how consumers react to having a choice between getting interest on their current accounts (as is the case in most European banks) but paying more for current bank operations like issuing cheque books, etc., or getting no interest (as with many French banks) but paying less for current operations and transactions.

It will also be interesting to see whether people's attitudes to saving and investing will change. Will the French start investing in British pension funds and the British in French real-estate portfolios? That will depend not only on a change or evolution in national preferences and traditions, but on the possibilities offered by the various Stock Exchanges. Contrary to the banking world, the European Stock Exchanges have not made a great deal of effort towards concerted action. As a matter of fact, unifying Stock Exchanges has not figured at all in the preparation of the Single Market, and the one EC directive which does exist only came into being because it was necessary to cover all the activities of banks, including their participation in the Stock Market through investment services.

Discussions have proceeded at ministerial level, through the European Council of Ministers. Agreement has practically been reached, giving all investment companies the right to set up subsidiaries or operate straight from home in all EC countries, remaining under the control of their own authorities – just like banks. Stock Market transactions, however, would be carried out according to the rules and under the control of the host country's authorities. One of the questions yet to be decided is whether investment companies should be obliged to become members of the Stock Exchanges of the countries where they operate.

Discussions on the rules that should or should not govern take-over bids have not come off and have little chance of doing so by 1993. So, for the moment, on that question existing national rules prevail – though individual investors and shareholders would be well advised to keep an eagle eye on future developments, if only through their brokers; they should also keep abreast of the decisions taken by the European Commission when it comes to allowing certain take-over bids to be made because the Commission is very careful to stop any move that could result in an eventual industrial monopoly.

Consumer protection when it comes to loans and credit is a question that has long been exercising the European authorities. As early as 1986, they adopted a directive stipulating that all credit contracts have to be done in writing and must mention the cost of the credit or the global annual interest rate. This directive covers all forms of credit – bank accounts, credit cards, personal loans, credit purchase, etc.

The next step will be to establish a vocabulary that can be understood by everybody, using in particular the same terms to designate the same things everywhere, thus allowing consumers to understand exactly what they are letting themselves in for, and to compare the real cost of the various credit offers.

The methods used to work out the cost of consumer credit will also be standardized by 1996, except for France and Germany, who have been allowed more time in which to adjust their own systems.

All this may seem very basic and elementary, but these first steps are indispensable to avoid people getting totally lost and confused by the avalanche of credit offers which may well engulf them after 1992; giving them the practical means of understanding is the only way to guarantee their right to choose and thus become the driving force of a market.

As stated earlier, the obligation to give preliminary explanations in writing extends to what could be termed 'everyday credit' – including cheques and credit cards. Throughout the EC, anybody opening a new current account and therefore getting a cheque book, or asking for a credit card, must be presented with a written document explaining such things as costs, interest rates (if any), the delay in debiting or crediting an account, the consequences of irregular or irresponsible use of the account, etc. Banks are also deemed responsible for the functioning of cash distributors.

The use of credit cards is rapidly developing throughout the Community, with two major networks: Visa and Eurocard/Mastercard. They are most widely used in France and the United Kingdom, with France galloping ahead of everybody else when it comes to the use of cheques. The Germans, strangely enough for such a business-oriented country, still prefer hard cash (or are they trying to tell us something?).

What is important, however, is the freedom to use whatever form of payment one wishes, thanks in particular to the growing number of cash points (30,000 throughout the EC in 1990), many of which will accept international credit cards.

Since exchange controls were abolished in 1990, the Europeans benefit from another facility: they can write a cheque in whatever EC currency they wish, using their own cheque book. So, the owner of a Barclays Bank cheque book can make out a cheque in Belgian francs, for instance, using one of his cheques. For the moment, this is not really accepted in shops, but is done quite normally in the case of international transactions, even simple ones like booking a room in a hotel in another EC country.

The one major drawback with this kind of facility is that banks tend to demand rather high transaction costs. This is something the EC authorities are looking into, and they may well end up by establishing a basic code of conduct for banks. After all, there is no real reason for banks to charge higher costs for a transaction between two EC countries than between two locations in the same country – the only difference is having to work out the exchange rate, which is done by a computer in ten seconds flat; apart from that, the amount of time and work needed are the same, now that all these transactions have been simplified. One cannot help suspecting that customers' lack of knowledge or unwillingness to make a fuss are being put to good use for upping the ante without justifiable reasons.

The ECU

It's at this point that the question inevitably and understandably crops up: what about the ECU then? Considering the vast amount of money wasted in currency exchanges and bank transactions (see page 47), wouldn't it be simpler and more cost-effective to use the European Currency Unit? Of course it would, and it is in fact possible for private individuals to use the ECU in a number of financial operations. Before going into details, it may be useful to know a few basic facts about the ECU itself and, by the same token, about the European Monetary System (EMS).

The EMS was officially set up on 13 March 1979; the aim of the member States was to create monetary stability within the Community by coordinating the various national economic and financial policies. This meant having a common code of reference – a measure of value, which led to the creation of the European Currency Unit as a means of payment between capital banks of the member States for transactions carried out in connection with the EMS.

It was therefore one of the main instruments of the EMS, the other being the Exchange Rate Mechanism (ERM) aimed at maintaining exchange parities between the various currencies so as to avoid some currencies suddenly doubling in value compared to others and being used for all kinds of speculative deals.

All member States belong to the EMS; not all adhere to the ERM.

The United Kingdom didn't until 1990, when John Major, then Chancellor of the Exchequer, 'anchored' the Pound to the Exchange Rate Mechanism. Until then, the Pound, even though it was valued against the ECU like the rest of the Community currencies, was free to soar or plummet on its own against all the other international currencies, like the Dollar and the Yen. The other EC currencies had to have their values adjusted against each other and it was this 'inter-European' value of each currency that was (and is) taken into consideration on the international markets. This means, for instance, that the Bundesbank cannot let the value of the Deutschmark go up in leaps and bounds to the detriment of the Franc, the Florin or, now, the Pound without getting a sharp rap on the knuckles from the other central banks; it then has to intervene on the Exchange Markets to stop speculation on the German currency.

The British were unwilling to join the ERM because they considered that the Pound was one of the world's basic reserve currencies – which the other European currencies were not – and should not therefore be shackled to a fistful of 'second rate' monies. Unfortunately for Britain, all this talk of international reserve currency was not mirrored by facts. Since the seventies, the Pound was being used less and less as reserve currency and didn't cover more than 2 to 3% of international reserve – in fact no more than the French Franc!

Even though the Pound did not participate in the ERM the UK did, and does, use the ECU in the same way as the other EC countries.

The ECU is made up of a 'basket' of the ten EC currencies; the value of each currency in connection with the ECU reflects its economical and financial importance.

AVERAGE ANNUAL RATE OF THE ECU (1988)

Belgian Franc/Luxemb. Franc	43.43
Deutschmark	2.07
Danish Crown	7.95
Drachma (Greece)	167.58
Escudo (Portugal)	170.06

French Franc	7.04
Florin (Netherlands)	2.33
Irish Punt	0.78
Lira (Italy)	1537.33
Peseta (Spain)	137.60
UK Pound	0.66
US Dollar	1.18
Yen	151.46

As with other currencies, the value of the ECU is determined on the foreign exchange markets; however, its originality lies in the fact that its value can also be calculated on the basis of the exchange rates of its ten constituent currencies. What does the ECU look like? Nothing at all, since it does not exist in the form of notes and coins. That does not stop it from being used in an increasing number of international transactions. It is among the five 'currencies' most often used for issuing international bonds.

Individuals can use ECU traveller's cheques within and without the Community; they can buy bonds in ECU, make deposits and, in some countries, obtain bank loans in ECU. Since July 1990, it has been possible to open bank accounts in ECU in eight out of the twelve member States.

Since the Maastricht agreements of 1991 the ECU is destined to become the European Community's single currency – with our national currencies like the Pound, the Franc or the Deutschmark just being different ways of naming the same thing, or perhaps even disappearing altogether in favour of European coins and banknotes. This idea is anathema to many UK politicians, who believe (or at least say) that a single European currency would mean the end of financial independence for the UK and that national budgets would actually be decided in Brussels. What they don't say is that in European countries, national budgets can in no way be worked out without taking into account such details as international trade, international money market evolution or upheavals, international political events – so an 'independent' national budget does not exist. Everybody knows that the reuniting of Germany and the quasi-automatic entry of its Eastern half into the European Community have had various consequences for the other EC economies, because Germany has had to readjust its own economic priorities.

In any case, monetary union is an avowed aim of the Single Act, and if the UK remains its only adversary within the Community, it will end up being in such an uncomfortable position that its only choice may be between opting out altogether or agreeing to go along with the others.

INSURING FOR
THE FUTURE

The field of insurance has really been one of the bloodiest battlefields of the Community.

It took twenty years for the Commission to obtain the slightest concession from the member States and even then – in 1977 – it only managed to do so by a sleight of hand which enabled it to appeal to the European Court of Justice against national restrictions and protectionist measures in the insurance sector. Of course, every time the question of insurance cropped up, what really worried the various governments was the question of tax: those countries where insurance policies are taxed were not at all keen to see their own nationals rush off to take out insurance policies in other EC countries where they are tax-free, just as they can freely open bank accounts there. Nor were they at all keen to give up the yearly millions of pounds' worth of money they got from these taxes.

Without going into complicated details, suffice to say that, in 1977, the Commission got the European Council of Ministers to adopt a 'technical' directive authorizing insurance companies to offer their services throughout the Community in the field of 'major risks'. This concerned only businesses and companies, not individuals. The Finance Ministers adopted the directive without giving too much thought to the consequences . . . upon which the Commission immediately took Denmark, France, Germany and Ireland to court, accusing the four countries of 'restrictive practices' and protectionism in that field. By 1986, the Court had given, in all four cases, a verdict in favour of the Commission and severely reprimanded the national governments for acting against the basic principles of the Treaty of Rome on the freedom of establishment and of trade throughout the Community.

The result was a distinct acceleration towards a greater freedom to sell and take out insurance policies, although it still benefits the business world rather than the individual. This, in all fairness to the national and European authorities, is because businesses are more capable of defending themselves than individuals – freedom for insurance companies is all very well, provided it is accompanied by some form of protection for the individual consumer.

For the moment, and since July 1990, companies employing more than 500 people and having a turnover of at least 24 million ECUs (some £15.6 million) have been authorized to take out insurance policies in whatever EC country they wished, except for life insurance and car insurance.

Then, as from January 1993, small and medium-sized enterprises (SMEs) employing more than 250 people and with a minimum annual turnover of 12 million ECUs (some £7.8 million) will also have an identical freedom of choice. All this, of course, is not ideal for countries where insurance policies are taxed. Which explains, for instance, why France has been cutting down or actually suppressing a certain amount of taxes, like the ones on fire insurance, and even on life insurance.

What is still in the process of being worked out is the right for an insurance company to offer its services in other EC countries without opening offices there, which means that it would be operating on the basis of the rules prevalent in its own country – just like banks. We're getting there, even if it's not very fast, but the problem should be sorted out by 1994. In June 1991, for instance, the Twelve decided that all insurance companies would be subject to common accountancy rules. This should allow a clear comparison of every company's yearly accounts, on a like basis, which means that clients, whether companies or individuals, should really be able to weigh their performances and their offers on identical scales.

Another way to ensure consumer protection will be to enable clients to really understand the contract they are being offered. It is sometimes difficult enough for an individual to understand a contract written in his own language – let alone in a foreign one! So, first of all, contracts will have to be submitted to clients in their own language, whatever the nationality of the insurance company. Secondly, clients who take out a policy in an EC country other than their own will be asked to sign a document stating that they understand and accept the fact that their policy is subject to the rules of the country where it has been issued. Thus a Briton taking out a policy with an insurance company in Hamburg will be made fully aware that the rules governing this policy are German rules. So, for the time being, a Briton who buys a house in France and contacts, say, the offices of the Norwich in Paris because his house in Britain is insured with the Norwich, will not be getting the same policy as the one he has in Britain. What he will get is a French contract in English, so that he can really understand all the clauses.

As for life insurance, that also is slowly moving towards a certain amount of inter-Community freedom. As, since 1990, people have been free to open bank accounts in whatever EC country they choose, it seems rather difficult to stop them using the money in those bank accounts to take out a life insurance in that country. So two different sets of rules have been devised to meet two different situations. If, for instance, a Frenchman or a Dane takes out a life insurance policy in Britain, that policy is governed by British rules. This is known as a 'passive freedom to offer services' because the insurance company was not, so to speak, peddling its wares in the client's native country.

If, however, an underwriter of the British insurance company goes to see the Frenchman or the Dane in their own countries, this is considered as an 'active offer of service' and the rules governing the policy will be those of the client's home country. Which is all very logical.

What it also means is that insurance companies cannot do the same thing as banks, i.e. offer services under the sole control and rules of their own country. Moreover it means that the whole situation is still rather complicated – and complicated situations are rarely in the interest of the client. So, thanks mainly to Sir Leon Brittan, one of the UK Commissioners in Brussels, the European Commission is working on yet another set of directives to try and simplify all this by establishing, as with banks, the right for an insurance company which complies with a few basic rules to set up offices or simply offer its services in another EC country without that country's preliminary authorization and to work under the control of its own country's authorities.

Finally, car insurance. For the moment, and until further notice, only companies will be able to take out car insurance wherever they wish. Individuals will go on taking out car insurance in their country of residence, knowing that this insurance covers them while travelling within the EC. In case of accident, their own company will sort things out with the company of any other vehicle driver involved.

TAXING QUESTIONS

Query: what is the difference between mankind facing the problem of death and the Twelve facing the problem of taxation? Answer: None. In both cases, everyone pretends it doesn't exist, but it always catches up with them in the end . . .

This rather gruesome joke has long been doing the rounds of the various Commission bureaux: tax appears to be the one great symbol of national sovereignty and none of the member States wants this situation to change until they find themselves with their backs to the wall. The fact that any fiscal decision can only be taken by unanimous vote, and not a majority one, doesn't really help to get things moving.

What does happen, however, is that a directive adopted in another field of Community endeavour will start causing distortions on the tax front, so everybody has to rush around stopping gaps, instead of taking positive and clearly thought-out decisions. For instance, take the case of abolishing exchange controls and allowing people to open bank accounts wherever they want in the Community. The net result, of course, is going to be that most people will be opening deposit accounts in the countries where they are subject to very little tax, if any. (The same for life insurance, when the time eventually comes.) This has already led certain countries to diminish tax on savings and investments, so as not to suffer too much from outside competition. This was the case in France, and led to very strong political unease within the ruling socialist party. After all, it went strongly against the whole socialist idealogy to decrease tax on capital while continuing to tax the product of work by means of fiscality on incomes.

The debate was not made any easier when, at long last, the Twelve came to an agreement of sorts on VAT. The various French governments, whatever their political positions, always preferred strong indirect taxation – such as high levels of VAT – to high income tax. So, not only is France one of the EC countries with the lowest income tax (and about half of the working population being exempted anyway), it is actually the country where VAT was devised (so if anybody has any remarks to make, they can be addressed directly to Monsieur Maurice Lauré, who thought it all out!) In June 1991, the twelve Finance Ministers agreed that the normal rate of VAT would be a minimum of 15%. As for the minimal rate, it would be 5%. However, in those countries where certain goods do not carry VAT (such as books or children's clothes in the UK), this will remain in the status quo, at least for the time being.

Normal VAT rates in France are 18.6%, so the 15% minimum rate is not a problem. Nevertheless, the next step is inevitably going to be the setting of a maximum rate, which the Commission would like to see limited at 20%. The maximum rate in France, on luxury items and cars, is above that, so the State stands to lose millions of Francs which it is going to have to find elsewhere. It is therefore less than enthusiastic, unless . . . the loss of VAT income is compensated by an automatic 15% tax on savings, But, at this point, Luxembourg is digging its heels in and refusing to change its current policy of taxless savings so, for the time being, everything is more or less at a standstill.

So how does this affect the individual taxpayer? Not a lot since his rate of income tax is still being decided by his national authorities and the average rate of VAT hasn't changed all that much, since most countries have it at a minimum rate of 15% anyway (except Spain and Luxembourg, who are having to hoist theirs up by three points).

The only question of immediate interest to private citizens is the gradual disappearance of customs control at borders within the EC which will eventually affect the payment of excise duties on such goods as cigarettes and alcohol. Eventually is the operative word: although these excise duties should normally, by 1993, be replaced by a tax included in the selling price, there again the member States are having trouble agreeing on the exact amount of this tax. Some countries, like Denmark, have a high excise on alcohol, while others, like Italy, have no excise on wine and aren't really very keen to have one. So the temporary solution has been to increase travellers' allowances, in alcohol and cigarettes.

On the whole, although taxation is such an important and vast field which affects everyone – or perhaps because of that – there isn't really all that much to report about it for the moment as far as the individual European is concerned. It will still be a matter of getting as much information as possible on the tax policies and regulations of any EC country other than his own where an individual is going to work, retire or buy property. Trying to get fair treatment under double taxation agreements is still going to be a complicated, frustrating and drawn-out business. Fiscal Europe is definitely in the pipeline, but we will be lucky if we see it working by the year 2000 . . .

The avowed aim of the European Commission is that one day a German company trading with a British one, or a Danish company doing business with an Italian one should be able to deal in exactly the same conditions as they would if they were all in the one country, unhampered by fiscal complications and red tape. But what about individual citizens? Will they live to see the day when they all find themselves paying income tax or VAT on the basis of the same criteria, wherever they choose to live and work within the Community?

That is the million ECU, tax deductible, question.

5 Healthy, wealthy . . . and wise?

Europeans are no different to the rest of humanity: they complain about the cost of living, the inadequacy of their financial conditions, the decline in quality of products and services . . . and about life in general. And yet, since the European Community was born, some thirty years ago, the people of the EC are twice as well off in terms of living standards. As for the Community itself, it is three times as rich as it used to be, which obviously entailed substantial improvements in working conditions, health services and social assistance of all sorts.

Having said that, it's only fair to point out that the twelve EC countries haven't progressed at the same rate: it's the less industrial, less developed countries which have benefited the most from the general improvement; that's to be expected, since they started off from further down the scale. As for the others, because they already have relatively well-organized systems of social protection, they tend to consider that what they've got is good enough and doesn't require improvement (as is the case for Germany) or else that too much social protection can be a hindrance to economic development (as with the United Kingdom). Not that the thrust towards better social protection was that much more noticeable elsewhere. In the so-called 'poorer' countries of the southern half of the EC, the authorities are not always madly keen to increase social protection to an extent that might discourage their more industrially developed neighbours from investing and creating jobs in these areas where labour is cheaper and workers less demanding. (For years the Anti-Slavery Society has been denouncing the abuse of child labour in Italy, for instance, and not getting much response . . .)

As it turns out, resisting social progress is rather a short-sighted way of looking at things: on the one hand, when it comes to 'cheap' labour Europe is largely outdistanced by other parts of the world, namely South-East Asia, and on the other, what more and more industries are looking for is a properly qualified workforce capable of rising to the challenge of sophisticated technology rather than industrial cannon-fodder – and this means spending more on education and vocational training.

The European authorities are faced with a double problem. You cannot have a Community where part of the people benefit from a satisfactory health, social security and worker protection system, while others have to make do with much less. There would be no point in having a Community under these conditions. On the other hand, you cannot get away from the fact that, out of an active population of some 150 million people, about 15 million, i.e. no less than 10%, are on the dole. So, what must the Community's priorities be: to help the unemployed find a job, or to give better protection to those who are lucky enough to be working while vaguely propping up those who aren't?

In the current social climate, the general and immediate response tends to be: let's start by creating jobs and, for the rest, leave well alone, or else things will become even more difficult for everyone.

That, however, is not the way the European Commission tackles the problem. The Commissioners cannot be pulling jobs out of a hat every five minutes – all they can do is work towards implementing the Single Market which should, if properly working, help create several million jobs and give Europe a much-needed economic impetus. What they can try to do – and are working very hard at – is to establish a certain amount of very basic rules for protecting people's health and working conditions, and to build bridges between the various national systems in such a way that a citizen of one EC country does not lose out if he is sent, or chooses to go, to work in another member State.

The Commission also has to work on the basis of existing

figures which distinctly show that, since the 1980s, the number of people joining the labour force has been regularly decreasing because of the general fall in the birthrate. This particular trend is not yet visible to the naked European eye mainly because it is hidden by the rise in unemployment. At this particular point in time, there is a conjunction of several elements which keep unemployment figures high – apart from the obvious fact that job creation is at a low point all over the Community (1.6 million new jobs between 1975 and 1987, as opposed to 26 million in the USA and 7 million in Japan).

To start with, the post-war 'baby-boom' generation is still very much there on the job market and will continue to work for another fifteen to twenty years. The second important phenomenon is the rising number of women on the employment market. It was particularly spectacular in the ten years between 1977 and 1987. In that period, within the EC (as we know it today, i.e. the twelve countries that are now members) the total active population grew by 18.7% out of which only 2% were men. And thirdly, the continual arrival of young people on a saturated market (even though their numbers decrease yearly) is making the unemployment figures rise in leaps and bounds. In the EC only one out of six jobs is held by a man or woman under the age of twenty-five. It isn't actually all that different from what's happening in the USA (one job in five for an under twenty-five) but is interesting to compare with Japan, where only one in eight jobs is held by an under twenty-five. And that's not due to lack of jobs; there's a reason most Europeans would do well to think about: longer schooling and vocational training, meaning more qualified workers, better capable of holding down their jobs.

However, while Europe is quite evidently being extremely backward in creating jobs, what is also going to become obvious in the next few years is the growing number of people retiring. What we are seeing now is nothing compared to what is going to happen in the next ten to fifteen years, when the 'baby-boomers' start taking their pensions. This is a problem the Commission is acutely aware of; it is convinced that now is the right time to work on protecting the rights of pensioners within the Community instead of waiting for the situation to become unmanageable.

But here, as with the rest, things are moving very slowly, if only because nobody can come to a permanent agreement on how European social measures should be adopted – whether by a unanimous or a majority vote (stop me if you've come across that one before . . .). Depending on the subject being discussed, some European partners will say that it comes directly under the heading of Article 100 of the Treaty of Rome stating that any decision liable to have a direct influence on the establishing and functioning of the Common Market can only be adopted by a unanimous vote; others will insist that, not at all, it comes under the heading of Article 100A, which allows a simple majority vote for questions concerning a better harmonization of working conditions within the EC.

As everybody has to start by agreeing on that particular point, progress, such as it is, has been achieved at a snail's pace and there is not much hope of things being sorted out by 1993. But, however slow, there actually has been some progress. Since December 1989, the Community is the proud owner of a Social Charter on which nearly all the member States have agreed, even though they are definitely taking their time about turning words into action.

FIGHTING UNEMPLOYMENT

Facts and figures

Unemployment figures in the EC went up spectacularly after the two oil crises of the 'seventies. In 1973, oil prices were multiplied by four, in 1979 by two. Since then, the rate of unemployment, having gone from 3.2% up to 11% of the active population, has more or less settled to around 10% as mentioned earlier. This rise gave birth to the terrible problem of long-term unemployment: 56% of all those on the dole have been unemployed for more than a year, a third for more than two years – the percentages are even higher in certain countries like France, Italy, the Netherlands and the United Kingdom.

Naturally, since these crises began, the Community authorities have not been sitting around doing nothing. There have been different stages and different types of action.

At the start, in the 'seventies, the member States began by putting their metaphorical heads together and comparing national policies. Having set up an exchange network of experiences and information, in 1974 they adopted a social action programme outlining emergency measures to be taken during the following three years. This consisted mainly in coordinating the efforts of the various national labour departments – ministries, quangos, etc. However, until June 1980, all the efforts to decrease unemployment retained a national character, with each country doing what it thought best for its own citizens; but at least, at decisional level, everybody who took the trouble to ask knew what everybody else in the Community was doing and thus tried (not very successfully) to avoid making the same mistakes as the others.

But, in June 1980, the European Council of Ministers agreed on the outline of a common EC policy on the question of unemployment, with definite aims and measures. This policy included, amongst other things, a study of the Community as a whole and not just as a patchwork of national situations; this implied a better practical cooperation and an exchange of immediately usable information between labour departments and also employment bureaux. For instance, since 1980, every three months employment bureaux in one EC country exchange detailed information with bureaux in the other countries on available jobs. If you go, say, to the Chamber of Commerce of an EC country in London, they normally have lists of certain types of jobs available to other EC nationals in that country. As not everyone can go posting off to London, local employment bureaux should be capable of making these lists available, providing one asks.

On a more general level, the European Council (of Heads of State) undertook, in 1982, to promote and encourage public and private investments, and to stimulate the development of small and medium-sized enterprises. This is obviously very far from the usual cliché that European social policy consists in encouraging trade unions to put spokes in the wheels of economic development. As Jacques Delors once said, there can be no social progress without economic progress and no economic progress without social cohesion.

Naturally, it was all very well to adopt resolutions and decide on measures and objectives but it then takes a certain amount of time to get things done. For instance, it wasn't until 1988 that the EC countries managed to put together a report pinpointing the measures which, in each member State, really helped fight against long-term unemployment.

Improvements

Simultaneously, the resources of the European Social Fund were increased to promote training schemes and create job opportunities for the young unemployed. The European Social Fund (ESF) had actually been in existence since 1960, when it was set up as prescribed in the Treaty of Rome. Its objective is to promote job facilities and professional mobility for workers throughout the Community – it is destined in particular to help the unemployed get back on to the labour market. To start with, the Fund didn't obtain many satisfying results, for two main reasons. First of all, projects were not funded in advance, but were paid for once they had been put into action, which was not terribly motivating. Secondly, because the objectives of the ESF were couched in rather general terms, the money was not distributed in a very rigorous way but went mostly to those countries who already had well-organized training structures and . . . the necessary preliminary funds. So the Fund was restructured on several occasions and, since 1990, it is aimed very specifically at contributing to programmes on vocational training for long-term unemployed and young unemployed (under twenty-five), especially in geographical areas where there are economic difficulties (regions where mines have closed down, for instance); apart from training, the Fund can also give financial help when it comes to setting up new businesses in that area.

At the same time, the Community got down to the business of giving a fairer share of help, in general, to those areas that needed it most. Until the mid-seventies, Community efforts tended to benefit the more central regions of Europe – those who had the more efficient networks of communication and distribution. As it happened, they were also amongst the richer areas – thus money went to money and the less developed areas were more or less left out in the cold. In 1975, the Community created the European Regional Fund, whose aim is to finance investments in the less favoured regions.

But what effect can this have on the individual European, when it comes to jobs? A very direct effect indeed: every year since 1975, some 60,000 jobs are created or saved thanks to the Fund.

As for the less direct effects, they are more difficult to measure, but are nonetheless very important. Let's take an example or two. In 1983 and 1984, the Fund contributed 7.8 million ECUs towards the building of a power station at Kozani in Macedonia, Greece, thus vastly increasing electrical supplies in that zone and therefore encouraging its economic development. In Belfast, Northern Ireland, the Fund is contributing 1.25 billion ECUs towards a complete programme of urban renovation including roads, hydraulic plants, modernization of the airport, development of trade; this programme should help, directly or indirectly, to improve the lives and working conditions of some half a million people.

And improvements are continuing. The Single Act specifically demands that the Commission prepare a vast reform of the structure of the Fund based on a greater efficiency and a better distribution of finances. This has in actual fact brought about an important reform in the Community's agricultural policy (see Chapter 11). So the farmers amongst us are also directly concerned.

On top of the various Funds, one of the most recent improvements has been the Social Charter. In September 1989, the European Commission adopted this 'European Charter of Fundamental Social Rights', put together thanks mainly to the work of the European Parliament and the Economic and Social Committee (see Chapter 10). It was then solemnly adopted by all members of the European Council – except the United Kingdom – in December 1989. Furthermore, according to the specifications of the Single Act, the Council asked the Commission to start working on the practical means of making the Charter work for the individual European.

THE SOCIAL CHARTER

A bit like Magna Carta, the European Social Charter lays down the fundamental rights and principles that must guide the social policies of the member States. Some of these principles must be implemented by the Community as a whole because they concern everybody at the same time; others are left to the various member States to decide how, when and in what order they shall be implemented on a national basis. Also, some of these principles are destined to help in the fight against unemployment, others to defend the rights of workers, of pensioners, of handicapped people.

They lay down:

– freedom of movement within the Community for anyone wishing to work in any of the member States. This freedom of movement is the major basic principle of the Community, whether it concerns working, living, travelling or trading;

– the right to social protection, i.e. to a minimum income for workers and appropriate social aid for those who are excluded from the labour market or who do not have adequate means of subsistence;

– the right to vocational training, whether before or during an individual's professional life;

– the right to a job and an adequate remuneration. This concerns part-time workers, who must be able to refer to an equitable minimum wage. It also includes the right to sufficient means of livelihood in the case of a salary being seized;

– the right to better living and working conditions. This clause of the Charter is aimed at harmonizing the conditions existing in the various member States, with a view to improving them. It concerns many aspects of people's work and life, including the amount and flexibility of working hours for all jobs (day jobs, night-time jobs, part-time jobs, weekend jobs, etc.), annual holidays, collective lay-off, judicial proceedings, etc.;

– the right to belong to a trade union, and the right to collective negotiation;

– equal rights between men and women, not only on the question of salary, but on those of education, vocational training, promotion, etc.;

– the right for workers to be informed and consulted on all events in the life of a company that may concern them directly or indirectly. This includes people working for a company or an organization that has plants, offices or subsidiaries scattered throughout various Community countries;

– the right to satisfactory security and health conditions within the place of work;

– protection for children and adolescents. This clause establishes that the minimum age to start work is sixteen and that young people must be guaranteed the same professional rights as adults;

– the right for a retired person to receive a pension or, failing that, a minimum income as well as social and medical care;

– the right for handicapped people to benefit from specific measures in such fields as training, and social and professional re-education.

Having established the principles – which is very important because it means the member States have agreed on a series of clauses that are going to determine the way their future social policies are decided – the question is now to establish what is actually being done by the Community in a practical way for various categories of the population.

MIGRANT WORKERS

Employed and unemployed

The EC regulations on social security for migrant workers aim at ensuring that, if you work in one or several member States other than your own, you can then combine social security contributions paid in each of these States in order to qualify for benefits. And, when the need arises, you must be able to obtain those benefits whatever the member State you are living in. This means that you do not lose out on your entitlements when you exercise your Charter-given right to work in another member State.

These regulations apply to employed and self-employed people and retired pensioners, as well as to their families.

Normally, you pay social security contributions in the member State where you are working, even if you usually live elsewhere. If you are sent to another member State temporarily, you may continue to be insured in your own country. 'Temporarily' in this case means one year maximum, although there is a provision for extending that period for up to two years. To secure this right, your employer (or you, if you are self-employed) should apply to the social security authorities using Form E101.

Rules and procedures change according to the different benefits. In general, the right to 'export' benefits only applies to those benefits which depend on your contribution record to a particular insurance scheme, such as National Insurance in the United Kingdom. It does not apply to means-tested benefits like income support or family credit. What usually happens is that the authorities of the country in which you claim will look at your contribution record *in that country* to see if you qualify for benefit there. If you don't, they will also look at your contributions in other member States to see if your combined records allow you to qualify.

As far as unemployment benefit is concerned, you can also qualify if you have paid contributions in two or more member States, but you must always start by applying in the country where you last contributed. You may transfer your benefits to another member State using Form E303, provided you have been receiving them for at least four weeks. At that point, you can ask the Department of Employment to have your benefits transferred to wherever you will be going in another Community country. When you arrive there, you must register as unemployed within seven days and then comply with local requirements when it comes to signing on. You will then receive your UK benefits paid to you each week for thirteen weeks – and not the local benefit, which may or may not be higher than yours.

After thirteen weeks, you are no longer entitled to benefit. You can then apply for a means-tested payment in the country where you are residing – although you may not necessarily qualify for it (it will depend on the country). As for unemployment benefit in the country concerned, you can apply only if you have contributed to social security in that country, which means that you must have worked there for at least a week.

Sickness and child benefit

You can also combine insurance paid in two or more member States in order to qualify for sickness benefit from the country where you are working. It's the country where you paid your last contribution that finances the benefit. You must apply to the social security authorities in the country where you fell ill. If you wish to have your benefit transferred (say, you want to return to the UK but are getting benefit from German social security) you must obtain an advance authorization from the country paying your benefit.

Concerning invalidity or disablement allowances, there again contributions paid in two or more member States may be combined to help you qualify for this payment. In some countries, invalidity pension is not linked to a specific number of years' insurance contributions, but is similar to disability benefit and is payable by the country where you were paying contributions when the invalidity occurred. In other countries it is like a retirement pension and therefore paid by all the countries where you stayed and worked on a proportional basis. You can have your benefit transferred provided you ask for prior authorization.

Under EC regulations, family allowances (i.e. child benefits) are paid by the member State where you are employed, even if your family is living in another State. However, if your spouse is working in that other State, child benefit will be payable there.

Finally, as stated earlier, EC regulations are linked to insurance contribution records and do not generally apply to social assistance or means-tested payments such as income support assistance. If you are living and working in a member State, you are eligible for all their social benefits – education, housing and social security. But you cannot transfer your entitlement to means-tested benefits from one member State to another. This means, as already stated, that you cannot transfer your entitlement to income support if you go to look for work in another member State.

The European Commission has also worked out a directive to protect the salaries and rights of migrant workers when they are detached by a company from their country to another EC state.

The directive stipulates that the employer who sends a worker to another EC country must respect the social rules of that country, especially if they are more advantageous for the worker. For instance, the minimum monthly wage in Portugal is 200 ECUs, while it is 757 ECUs in France. What the Commission wants to avoid is 'social dumping', i.e. a Portuguese company detaching some of its employees to France while still paying them Portuguese wages. They will have to be paid whatever French workers get for an equivalent job. This is to protect the Portuguese workers, but also French workers and French companies against disloyal competition. These measures don't concern just wages, but also working conditions, racial or sexual discrimination, etc.

Pensions and retirement

The EC regulations on social security for migrant workers aim to ensure that, if you work in two or more Community countries, you will be able to combine state pension contributions paid in each State in order to qualify for benefits and that you will be able to have your state pension paid in whichever member State you choose to live.

Normally, you must pay social security contributions in the country where you work, even if you live elsewhere. If you live in one Community country, and work both there *and* in another member State, you will normally be subject to the National Insurance scheme of the country where you reside. However, if you work in two or more Community countries but do not live in any of them, you will normally contribute to the scheme of the country where you do most of your work. This means that when you eventually claim your pension in one member State, your pension contributions in another State are not credited to the pension authorities of that State in which you have claimed; your pension will usually represent a proportion of the full pension you would be entitled to in each country where you have worked, had you stayed there; this proportion takes into account the number of years you actually worked in each country. In other words, each country where you worked pays you part of your pension, and it all adds up to a whole.

There is no such thing as a European Community pension. If you have paid contributions in two or more member States, you may qualify for a part-pension from each of them. Each country assesses your entitlement in two ways and then pays you the larger amount. This needs a bit of explaining, so settle down comfortably before I begin.

For instance, if you have worked for ten years in the UK and twenty years in France, the UK Department of Social Security will:

– calculate what pension you would get on the basis of your UK contributions alone, which represent a third of your total contributions; then, separately,

– add up the contributions paid in both countries, and divide that number by three, since you worked for one-third of your professional life in the UK. They compare the two amounts, i.e. pension based on your UK contributions alone against pension based on one-third of your total contributions, and pay you the largest of the two amounts.

Meanwhile, back at the local Département de Sécurité Sociale, the French are doing exactly the same thing: comparing a pension based on your French contributions alone to a pension based on two-thirds of your total contributions during your working life. They will also pay you the higher of the two amounts. Some people have all the luck . . .

Anyway, you will be receiving two part-pensions, a British one and a French one, which will be paid to you directly in the country where you are living. The whole idea is that a migrant worker's pension should be based on his contributions, not his nationality, even if, had he never moved, he would be getting a smaller pension in his own country.

Since the end of 1991, pensioners can retire in any EC country they wish and benefit from Community rules even if they never worked in that country. They will however have to provide proof of adequate financial means and health insurance contributions.

When pension rights have been acquired in another member State *before* the United Kingdom joined the Community, these periods will be governed by the national law and international agreements that existed at that time. The same applies if you worked in member States before they joined the EC (Ireland or Portugal, for instance).

A widow may combine contributions paid by her husband in two or more member States in order to qualify for a pension if the contribution record in one country only is not sufficient. The amount payable is worked out in the same way as for retirement pensions. The same applies, naturally, to widowers.

Periods of employment outside the Community may be recognized by one of the member States in which you are claiming, but do not have to be recognized by the others. If, for instance, you have worked in France, in Sweden and in the UK, your contributions in Sweden may be recognized by the UK authorities but not by the French – which is only natural, since these contributions should be taken into account by only one of the EC countries' Social Security departments, not by both.

How do you claim your pension? Either from the country in which you are now living, or from the country in which you last worked. When you make your claim, you will be asked for details of your work in other member States (e.g. period of employment or self-employment, salary or gains, etc.). Your local pension body will verify these claims with the relevant body in the other EC country (or countries) where you worked, and then calculate, as already explained, the amount you are entitled to, payable partly by every country where you worked. Your local pension authorities will explain how payments are to be arranged.

While your claims are being investigated, if you have reached pensionable age, you will normally be entitled to a pension from the country in which you live until your final pension is determined.

If you wish to delay receiving part of your pension because, for instance, in one country where you worked you get a lower entitlement at sixty-two than at sixty-five, it may be possible for you to defer payment until a later date and just receive the pension from the country in which you are living. This however remains a matter of national rules, and details should be sought out with the relevant authorities well in advance.

Following the Barber case (see page 72), the idea of a retirement age that would apply throughout the EC is gaining ground. The European Commission has also suggested an EC 'over-sixties' card, aimed at getting this age group better facilities in transport and travel, and in cultural activities. Finally, 1993, first year of the Single Market, has been designated 'European Year of the Elderly and of Solidarity between Generations'.

WOMEN'S RIGHTS AND EQUAL OPPORTUNITIES

The main problem facing women in the European Community has been identified as that of equality: equality with men at work and equal opportunities in society. The EC Treaty stipulates that men and women should get equal pay for equal work. To date the EC has adopted five directives to implement this general principle.

1. In 1975, the first directive made it an obligation to apply the principle of equal pay for work of equal value. It provides legal guarantees for the enforcement of this right and protects employees against dismissal resulting from discrimination.

2. In 1976, the second directive on equal treatment at work prohibited all sex-based discrimination at work. By implication it guarantees equal treatment with regard to recruitment, vocational training and promotion.

3. In 1979, the third directive on equal treatment in social security matters was aimed at achieving equality for women in statutory social security schemes.

4. In 1986, the fourth directive ensured equal treatment in

occupational social security schemes.

5. In 1986 again, the fifth directive applied the principle of equal treatment to the self-employed, including those working in agriculture.

The effect of the EC Treaty and the adoption of the directives has been to create specific Community rights against sex discrimination. These rights may be enforced in national courts and in employment tribunals without having to appeal through Brussels.

The majority of part-time workers in the Community are women. Their working conditions give them less job security and they are often paid less for the same amount of work than men who do an equivalent job full-time. In two recent decisions, the European Court of Justice ruled that treating part-time workers differently to their full-time colleagues will often be indirect discrimination against women. In one case, a German law relieving an employer from the obligation to make sickness payments to an employee who worked less than ten hours a week was struck down. In another case, the European Court ruled that a local authority could not refuse part-time staff (of which 90% were women) a severance grant on retirement that was given to full-time employees. Different treatment of part-time employees must be justified by the employer.

In another case, in 1988, the Court made it easier to prove that an employer is unfairly discriminating against women by placing on the employer himself the onus of showing that any difference in treatment is not based on the sex of the employee.

In the UK, legislation has been passed to implement the third directive on equal treatment in statutory social security schemes, although the Equal Opportunities Commission has challenged certain aspects of this legislation on the ground that it does not implement the directive in full.

While Community law allows member States to have different ages for men and women to receive a state pension, the European Court has established that public sector employees, such as health authorities and schools, cannot oblige women to retire at a different age to men. Also, even though state pensions may be payable at different ages, pensions under private company schemes must be paid to men and women at the same age. The same is true for all redundancy payments. This principle applies equally to men, so that they are guaranteed the same treatment on redundancy as women of the same age.

In one case (Barber, 1988), the European Court ruled that a man aged fifty-five, who was not eligible for a pension on redundancy under a company's rules concerning a private pension scheme before normal retirement age, was entitled to a pension, because a woman of the same age would have been eligible under the same scheme.

As part of the Commission's action programme implementing the Social Charter, it has proposed a directive in favour of the same maternity rights throughout the Community. If the directive becomes law, it will introduce a minimum fourteen-week period of leave with no loss of or reduction in pay. In addition, women in the UK would no longer be required to work two years for the same employer before qualifying for maternity leave and for protection from dismissal.

The Commission has also adopted a proposal protecting the dignity of men and women at work. It consists of a code of practice for employers, trade unions and workers on the means to fight sexual harassment, considered as one of the obstacles to a proper integration of women on the labour market.

The EC has set up bodies responsible for promoting equal opportunities.

– The Bureau for questions concerning employment and equal treatment of women monitors the application of existing directives in every member State. It also ensures that the principle of equal treatment is taken into account in other Community policies, such as education, training or programmes for small businesses.

– The Advisory Committee on Equal Opportunities for Men and Women helps the European Commission draft its equal opportunities policies and promotes the exchange of experience between member States.

– The Information Unit for Women, as its title indicates, is there to keep women throughout the Community informed on equal opportunities developments on an EC level but also in the various member States. It publishes a bi-monthly newsletter.

The EC has now launched into a further action programme

that should lead to greater legal rights, thanks to new directives on the burden of proof, parental leave and social security schemes, as well as new schemes to protect women in the field of vocational training and employment.

PROTECTION FOR
THE DISABLED

There are about 30 million people in the Community suffering from some form of physical or mental handicap. Measures to help their integration have been under way since the first action programme for the disabled in 1981, but the Social Charter and its programme have made it even more urgent to integrate them in the workforce.

Main activities for disabled people are grouped under the **Helios** programme. This programme outlines a certain number of key policies. On 12 June 1989, the European Council of Ministers invited the member States to uphold and continue their efforts to promote the integration of disabled people. The European Commission undertook to give the Helios Liaison Group information on VAT, new technology and driving licences and to improve coordination between its various departments on all matters that are of direct or indirect interest to the handicapped.

This is an application of the Social Charter, which states that all disabled persons, whatever the origin or nature of their disablement, must be entitled to concrete measures aimed at improving their social and professional integration. These measures, says the Charter, must concern in particular, according to the capacities of the beneficiaries, vocational training, ergonomics, mobility, means of transport and housing.

The Helios programme includes a computerized information system operating in all EC languages and dedicated to the problems of the handicapped, known as **Handynet**. It contains a database inventory of technical aids for the handicapped and a list of public and private organizations concerned with the production and allocation of these aids. There is a coordination centre in each of the twelve member States for collecting data.

Helios also gave rise to the Council resolution of May 1990 in which member States were encouraged to integrate disabled pupils into the ordinary education system wherever possible and to ensure that all education establishments can cater for their needs.

More specific actions concern:

– the Community network of vocational training and rehabilitation centres and experiences, with conferences, seminars, training sessions and study visits. There are fifty of these centres throughout the Community;

– a 1991 proposal for a directive to improve transport for workers with reduced mobility. This proposal covers public transport, as well as transport organized by employers and special services for the disabled;

– the promotion of independent living: access to public buildings and services, special equipment and home support services for private housing. The first European conference on independent living for disabled people was held in Brussels; prizes were awarded for outstanding developments in these areas;

– coordination in creativity and sport. An organization, **Eucrea**, has been set up to link national bodies aiming to stimulate artistic creativity among the disabled. In sport, the main activity has been the Special Olympics for the mentally handicapped held in Glasgow, and the World Games for the disabled in the Netherlands;

– *Documentation*. The Helios magazine for the disabled and those working with them now has a circulation of some 45,000;

– exchanges for young disabled people, to provide language and other types of training, in particular through the already established educational programmes like Petra, Lingua or Erasmus.

The **Horizon** programme, set up by the Commission in 1990, offers Community grant aid to people with a serious handicap resulting from physical or mental impairment, or to those suffering from other difficulties which hinder their economic or social integration. The aid covers vocational training for the handicapped and for those who work with them; the creation of small enterprises to create employment for the handicapped; starting up services or projects.

Tide is the socio-economic programme on Technology for the Integration of the Disabled and Elderly. It covers collaborative development work on several aspects of technology: consensus development and application for the working environment;

communications technology; control technology; integrated systems technology; innovation in rehabilitation technology; manufacturing techniques.

MEDICAL CARE

Treatment for travellers

Reciprocal health services are available within the EC countries; emergency treatment is provided to EC nationals on the same conditions as for each country's nationals. However, not all are provided free. It will depend on the system in use within each country. In some, medical treatment is free, in others part of the cost must be met by the patient, in others still, the whole treatment must be paid for pending a full or partial refund.

The careful traveller should never be without his Form E111, which entitles him to urgent medical treatment and medical care in case of illness in any EC State. If the aforementioned careful traveller is British, he can do without the E111 if he is going to the Republic of Ireland, to Denmark, Portugal or Gibraltar. The form is available in any main Post Office, and comes with a booklet bearing the rather Star-Warsy title of T2, which gives a certain amount of information on medical care while travelling in the EC. The first important piece of preliminary information is that if the counter clerk does not stamp and sign the E111 form before delivering it, there won't be much point in waving it about in a European surgery or hospital because it will be worthless. If, as is usually the case with us blasé and seasoned travellers, no one has thought about getting an E111 and a medical emergency occurs in another EC country, all is not lost. Following the instructions of the London Offices of the European Commission – Background Report ISEC/B17/91 – the forgetful traveller rushes off (or gets himself carried) to the local Health Insurance Authorities of the country concerned and asks them if they would kindly get hold of an E111 form by sending an E107 form to the Social Security Overseas Branch in Newcastle. It may be a good idea to provide them with the address (see page 206). . . .

Form E111 only covers temporary stays abroad, i.e. less than one year, and is only valid for those who live in the UK; it covers only urgent treatment for accidents or an unexpected illness.

You must apply for a refund before leaving the country you were visiting. It you leave your claim until you get back to the UK you may not get anything back, or, at the very least, have to face a very long wait. In any case, the system only applies to state health care schemes, not to private treatment.

Beware that EC medical arrangements do not necessarily cover every type of care, so check your own insurance in case you have to cover some of the cost yourself. This is particularly relevant when it comes to repatriating someone in case of illness or death. That cost is never covered by normal medical arrangements.

If you need medical care while visiting an EC country on business, your employer will generally pay you for the first twenty-eight weeks of illness, but not the cost of medical treatment.

Form E111 will not cover you if you go to another EC country specifically for medical or maternity care, or if you intend getting treatment while you are there. What you will need is Form E112 so as to obtain the authorization of the Department of Health. You will also need to send the Department a letter from your NHS hospital consultant recommending that you seek treatment in that other country, and describing the treatment required. If the Department approves it will send you back Form E112; without it, you will have to pay the full cost of any treatment you receive.

Medicines

If you need to take prescribed medicines while visiting another EC country, check on their availability in that country, as your doctor can only prescribe a limited amount under the NHS.

Normally, EC citizens are allowed to carry medicine from one Community country to another, provided they also carry the relevant prescription. Of course, there is always the question of medicines that can be bought over the counter . . . In the normal course of events, customs or security officials rarely get over-excited at discovering a couple of aspirins while checking our sponge bags for bombs in our deodorant sprays and heroin in our toothpaste tubes. It can nevertheless be a problem, because certain drugs are bought freely in some countries while requiring a prescription in others. Hence the need to check beforehand.

Another problem is the difference in prices from one country to another: drugs are usually more expensive in Germany, the Netherlands or the UK than in France, Spain or Italy, sometimes by a very wide margin (three times more in Germany than in Spain for certain types of medicine). But what can you expect when you have twelve different types of health systems and something like three thousand different companies manufacturing medical supplies within the EC?

Since 1986, however, the Community has been able to start harmonizing the manufacturing and trading of drugs, on two counts. Firstly, medicine which is the product of high technology or biotechnology is submitted for acceptance to a special Committee of Pharmaceutical Specialities which groups national authorities and Commission representatives, and bases its decisions on an evaluation report. As such medicines will represent more than half the EC production by the year 2000, we are all well on the way to an effective harmonization.

The second measure stipulates that if a product has been accepted and approved by one or more EC countries, then it must be allowed for sale in all the others within four months. This is known as the multi-State procedure.

But the Commission wants to take stronger steps and has suggested some new measures for 1993 and after, such as:

– giving certain drugs a purely national registration, which will mean that they can only be sold in the country where they are produced. This is aimed at protecting the smaller drug manufacturing companies, who cannot produce in vast quantities for the whole European market and would not be able to face the competition if similar drugs to theirs were sold in their country, coming from abroad;

– creating a European Drugs Agency, with a permanent Secretariat and several multinational specialist committees, whose mission it will be to decide whether or not a medicine can be put on the market throughout the EC, and whose decisions will be mandatory within thirty days. The Agency would also have the very important function of watch-dog – keeping a very strict tally of possible secondary effects of a drug and taking the appropriate action. Finally, it would also act as referee in case of disagreements between countries on the acceptance or refusal of a drug.

Everybody has agreed that such an Agency is indispensable.

The problem, as usual, is that nobody can agree on where the main offices of the Agency should be set up . . .

Blood

A very important directive was adopted in 1989, concerning blood transfusions and blood-derived medicine, in the wake of the AIDS problem. This directive stipulates that there must be a very strict control system at production stage (for drugs) and a series of rigorous tests on quality and security before the product is marketed.

Apart from this, the Commission is aiming at decreasing the danger of transmitting AIDS through the blood by obtaining agreement from the various States that they all go for free blood donations (instead of paying for them, which attracts drug addicts); it is also aiming at getting enough people to give blood for the Community to become self-sufficient. That would imply far more blood-donating campaigns than there are now.

Smoking

After January 1993, cigarettes containing more than 15 milligrames of tar will not be allowed for sale within the Community. When you consider that the French Gauloises have got 19.8 mg, Celtiques 23 mg and Gitanes Maïs 44 mg, you can imagine the mood in France at the loss of a long-cherished poison . . . Fear not, however, you devotees of brown tobacco cigarettes, the French National Tobacco Company is already preparing the appropriate product with less tar but with, apparently, the same taste!

Those who have bravely avoided or given up smoking will be pleased to learn that the European Council of Ministers has decided to forbid smoking in public places – schools, hospitals, cinemas, etc. Smoking on public transport is a decision left to each national authority.

When it comes to publicity, the Commission would like it to be confined to the written press – with the exception of children's magazines, of course – and always accompanied by the well-known warning about the danger to health. The European Parliament has actually voted against any publicity anywhere and in any form, direct or indirect (like sponsoring sporting activities).

Tobacco is not the only dangerous product the Community is worried about. All those that can cause domestic accidents are also being carefully monitored through a Community hospital network known as EHLASS – a rather appropriate abbreviation for European Home and Leisure Accident Surveillance System.

The question of dangerous toys, for instance, has already been studied, and appropriate measures taken (see Chapter 7).

Finally, by 1995, the whole of the Community should be linked by the same emergency telephone number: 112. This would mean that if you are in another Community country and need to make an emergency call, you don't have to dial the national number (such as 999 in the UK), though it will still be in use. All you have to do is dial 112 and your call will be put through to someone speaking your language who will liaise with the appropriate emergency services. And if that's not a wise European measure, what is?

EUROPEAN QUALITY LABEL

In December 1991, EC Environment Ministers agreed to introduce a community-wide 'eco-label' – a four-leaf daisy with the 12 stars and the letter E – designed for consumers to identify products that do the least damage to the environment. This label is intended to harmonize standards in the wake of increasing numbers of national labels and sometimes questionable 'environmental' advertising.

This scheme is voluntary, with the Commission setting standards by means of a regulatory committee made up of experts from the member States, and in consultation with consumer groups, environmental lobbies, industry and commerce. Product groups governed by separate legislation, like food, pharmaceuticals or dangerous chemicals are not involved.

6 Going green for Europe

The Single Act states that:

1) Action by the Community relating to the environment shall have the following objectives:

– to preserve, protect and improve the quality of the environment

– to contribute towards protecting human health

– to ensure a prudent and rational utilization of natural resources.

2) Action by the Community relating to the environment shall be based on the principles that preventive action should be taken, that environmental damage should as a priority be rectified at source, and that the polluter should pay. Environmental protection requirements shall be a component of the Community's other policies.

'How reassuring to know that the radioactive clouds sweeping over Europe from Chernobyl stopped short and turned back at the Franco-German border. . . .' This sarcastic comment was one of many made by the French press when it became clear that the attitude of the French authorities following the April 1986 explosion at the Chernobyl nuclear plant was going to be one of vaguely embarrased silence on a) the possibility of something similar happening in France and b) the actual fall-out over French territory (as over the other European countries) after that specific disaster, as if the Soviet Union were on another planet.

In truth, the attitude of the French government was no better but no worse than that of its European counterparts, if only because there really wasn't much anybody could do, except check and counter-check national systems. Natural – and, as in this case, unnatural – disasters have always had this nasty habit of not paying the slightest bit of attention to those barriers put up by humans that only manage to keep humans out.

Just seven months later, in November 1986, an explosion in a chemical plant near Basel, in Switzerland, poisoned the waters of the Rhine as it passed through Germany, France and the Netherlands on its way to the North Sea. Fishes in their thousands, and many other types of aquatic fauna, were destroyed.

Coming on top of other environmental 'incidents', like the acid rain over German forests, the Seveso dioxine leaks in Italy, the *Amoco Cadiz* shipwreck on the Brittany coast – to name but a few of the more spectacular ones – the 1986 ecological disasters were the utter limit, as far as Europeans were concerned. And they had yet to discover the appalling situation in Eastern Europe which, since the fall of the Berlin Wall in 1989, is turning out to be an unending succession of environmental massacres.

1986, as it happens, was also the year when the Single Act officially included the protection of the environment as one of the objectives for 1993 and beyond, thus giving the Community, for the first time, a legal text on which it could base its actions for the future. This of course does not mean that the Community had done nothing until then.

Any number of measures have been taken over the years, especially since 1972 when, following the first United Nations conference on the environment in Stockholm, the EC Heads of State gathered in Paris pointed out that economic expansion should also entail a better quality of life, in particular via a greater protection of the environment. They also asked the Community authorities to set up a first environmental action programme for 1973.

Unfortunately, 1973 happened to be the year of the first petrol crisis, with its subsequent economic recession. Not the best of times to start demanding expensive environmental discipline from an already harassed industrial world. Nevertheless, the Community persisted and in 1973, then in 1977, the first two environmental programmes were elaborated. What was typical of these programmes, as opposed to the policies followed in the eighties, was their essentially *corrective* character: in other words, they were dedicated to solving already existing problems, while the 1983 programme and following concentrated more and more on preventive action.

ADAPTING POLICIES TO MULTIPLE SITUATIONS

Because there is such a variety of climatic, geographical and economic situations within the EC, the number of ecological problems is as vast as it is diversified. Just to give you an idea, there are 300 different types of soil, more than 200 different types of countryside, some 6,000 varieties of plant life, around 100,000 species of invertebrates and nearly 600 types of birdlife.

The danger to wildlife is more important in the 'new' member States like Spain and Portugal because of the drive towards economic expansion, while air, water and coastal pollution is more serious in the industrialized areas of the Community. According to a 1986 report on the state of the environment, pollution due to phosphorus, petrol and nitrogen is growing in the North Sea area, as is the concentration of heavy metals near the Dutch coast, while the Mediterranean is consistently suffering from 'accidental' discharges, even though the level of contamination of sea organisms by pesticides and the like is decreasing.

The report also points out that, while certain types of atmospheric pollution are regressing, in particular smoke and sulphur, others, such as hydrocarbons, nitrogen and carbon dioxide, are progressing.

And this is just within the Community. If you add to all that the problems that concern the planet, such as the famous greenhouse effect, the destruction of tropical forests, desertification, etc., the EC can't worry only about its own situation, it must become an important part of all international bodies dedicated to the protection of the environment.

What is absolutely obvious is that environmental decisions have got to be taken at Community level – even if it means setting standards that are still difficult to reach for a certain number of the member States. It's not just a question of moral judgement – although the fact that one Community country can make use of another as a dustbin for its nuclear waste is creating more and more indignation – it is also a question of economic interests. National environmental standards are a very effective obstacle to free circulation of goods, and can cause unfair competition between European companies, if some are subject to greater environmental costs than their equivalents in other EC countries.

As a matter of fact, public opinion in Europe is demanding a global environmental policy. An opinion poll organized in 1990 for the European Commission in the twelve member States gave some very significant results.

It is well worth taking a look at the figures. To the question: 'should the member States act together or separately to protect the environment?' the answers (in percentages) were the following:

	Together	Separately	Don't know
Belgium	61%	8.6%	30.5%
Denmark	70.4%	12%	17.6%
France	80.6%	15.9%	3.5%
Germany (Fed. Rep.)	83.2%	5.7%	11.1%
Greece	69%	18.4%	12.6%
Ireland	64.4%	29.1%	6.5%
Italy	83.3%	7.7%	9%
Luxembourg	83.7%	11.6%	4.7%
Netherlands	91%	7.2%	1.8%
Portugal	62.3%	10.2%	27.5%
Spain	60.5%	19%	20.5%
UK	76%	16.5%	7.5%
Total	77.2%	12.2%	10.6%

Public opinion didn't express itself through opinion polls only. In the June 1989 European elections, the Green parties won more than thirty seats in the Euro-Parliament, thus becoming the fifth political group in that assembly. They would probably have won an even bigger number of seats if it hadn't been for the electoral systems applied in certain countries, like the UK, that are not favourable to the smaller parties.

As a typical example of European environmental policy based on the 1983 programme, a directive was adopted in 1985, submitting the construction of all vast industrial and infrastructural projects to a preliminary report specifying their possible impact on the environment. The European Commission also set up, in 1987, the **ACE** programme (Actions Communautaires pour l'Environnement) to finance individual projects based on 'clean' technology, the recycling of waste and new ways of protecting the quality of the environment.

The 1987–92 programme went another step further, since it included the protection of the environment as an essential element in all the Community's economic and social policy. This means systematically integrating the environmental angle in all decisions concerning industry, transport, tourism, energy, etc. For instance, the Commission itself has set up a series of procedures enabling it to make sure that all projects financed by its regional or agricultural funds are compatible with the demands of environmental protection. This has already led to reorienting the agricultural and transport policies of the Community.

The Commission, considering that protection also implies a thorough knowledge of the ecological situation, has proposed the creation of a European Environment Agency. The object of this Agency would be to collect and distribute all scientific and technical data that may come in useful when deciding on specific policies. It is destined to become the nerve centre of the existing national and regional network of environmental institutions, thus bringing together all the means of surveillance of Europe's natural environment. One of its most effective weapons will be an environmental data bank that is in the process of being elaborated.

One of the questions exercising the Commissioners is how to make sure that the Agency would be guaranteed total independence, i.e. the possibility of obtaining information from all types of sources. After all, the temptation to hide or minimize an ecological problem for all sorts of reasons has sometimes proved to be overwhelming, here and there throughout the world; national defence and national security are still powerful obstacles in the search for the environmental and health consequences of certain industrial or military initiatives.

The preventive strategy of the Community also implies stricter industrial and manufacturing standards. This means, of course, a general investment in favour of better quality and less polluting products. One of the best-known initiatives of the Community in this field was the 1985 directive (modified 1987) concerning lead-free petrol for cars. This directive fixes the maximum amount of lead at 0.4 to 1.5 grams per litre and has made it obligatory for all member States to ensure the distribution and sale of lead-free petrol as from 1 October 1989.

Another instance, in that same field, is the long-standing debate on 'clean' cars, i.e. the reduction of exhaust fumes by about 60 to 70% . The new standards, applicable in 1993, will be the same as those already compulsory in the USA and Japan since the beginning of the 'eighties. This will involve small cars (less than 1,400 cc), but the Commission has already submitted similar proposals for medium and large vehicles (for details see page 10).

Financing preventive policies is not limited to the ACE programme. There are several more. The European Investment Bank, for instance, will grant loans for installing waste-disposal or water-purifying systems, or for projects to ensure a purer atmosphere, or better sound-protection, etc.

The European Regional Fund also finances similar projects, in particular a programme known as **Envireg**, aimed at getting rid of pollution in a certain number of coastal regions, especially the Mediterranean. The problem, of course, is that, while the Mediterranean is not surrounded only by Community countries, its pollution problems must be treated as a whole. So another programme, **Medspa**, has been set up to deal specifically with the pollution of the Mediterranean within and without the boundaries of the Community.

The Commission is also thinking in terms of a European Environment Fund which would enable it to extend its financial interventions. It has already allowed national authorities, within certain limits, to attribute financial aid to industries who invest in anti-pollution measures. This, however, cannot go too far because, as stated in the official document, one of the principles of the Single Act is that 'the polluter should pay', not the taxpayer.

Keeping the public informed as much as possible is an important weapon in the fight to protect the environment, especially when it comes to taking preventive action.

Environmental groups do not have the same degree of organization and power all over the Community, but they are nonetheless a force to be reckoned with everywhere. The Commission has therefore submitted to the Council of Ministers a proposal aimed at facilitating the access of citizens to information being held by the authorities responsible for the environment on the one hand and, on the other, encouraging the authorities to publicize all relevant information on a wider scale than they do now. This should enable the individuals concerned to have a clearer understanding of the possible effects of such and such an initiative taken by national or local authorities – should they disapprove of these initiatives, they should also know enough to be able to defend their own point of view or their own environmental interests.

Naturally, the more knowledge one has of specific ecological problems, the more it becomes obvious that the whole question is a delicate and complex one, where many diverging points of view have to be taken into account, many often legitimate interests have to be upheld, where one cause can have many effects, etc. So, Community programmes must combine a diversified approach with excellent coordination. Otherwise, the danger will be that of pollution 'transfers' – that of nuclear waste disposal from one area to another is a typical, but not isolated, example.

Finally, the Commission is keen to solve a very difficult problem: the lack of enthusiasm of member States when it comes to applying Community decisions at a national level. There are something like 200 legislative texts adopted at Community level on environmental issues. A vast number of them have still not been applied in the member States. This means the Commission has to appeal time and again to the European Court of Justice against such and such a recalcitrant State. In view of this, the Commission wants to establish a certain number of mechanisms aimed at stimulating a proper application of Community legislation, in particular thanks to more direct contact between the EC institutions and the national organizations directly involved in environmental decisions.

CONSERVATION ISSUES

Protecting the natural heritage

This objective implies a more rational management of Community territory, subjected to an inordinate amount of industrial and agricultural development. Eighty per cent of the land within the twelve member States is given over to agriculture or to forests. The many research and study programmes undertaken under the aegis of the Community have led, amongst other things, to a ban on the use of certain pesticides, and to specific rules on the use of mud filters in agriculture.

The Commission's fourth programme includes various measures aimed at fighting the main causes of damage to soil, such as contamination by dangerous substances, erosion, improper or inefficient use of the soil. For instance, limits will be put on the quantity of chrome contained in mud filters for agricultural use.

In 1987, a five-year programme for the protection of forests against fire and acid rain was put into action.

On a world-wide level, the Community is set on developing a strategy to preserve tropical forests, and thus try to establish some sort of protection against the infamous greenhouse effect, and also help combat the extinction of many living species. Which is why the EC has signed the international convention against the buying and selling of threatened animal species. Importing the pelts of baby seals and ivory from elephant tusks has been banned throughout the EC.

In 1988, the Commission submitted a proposal aimed at protecting the natural habitat as well as the fauna and flora of Europe. Financial aid has already been given to initiatives for the preservation of certain threatened animal species like the Bonelli eagle, the wolf or the brown bear.

The fight for clean water, pure air, less noise

Water. Several European directives are concerned with the protection of underground and surface water, be it salted or unsalted. Different quality norms have been set out for the various categories, such as bathing water, drinking water, unsalted water fit for fish life, water used for breeding shell-fish and molluscs.

A certain number of dangerous substances have been put on 'black' or 'grey' lists, depending on how toxic they are. Substances that are on the black list (around 130 of them) are subject to a total ban, i.e. it is forbidden to let them anywhere near running water, under or above ground. If the relevant purification systems do not yet exist or are insufficient, then the elimination of these dangerous substances (mercury or cadmium, for instance) must be carried out under strict surveillance.

The Community has also issued specific instructions on the control and gradual reduction of industrial waste material containing titanium dioxide, known as 'red mud'.

It is also taking measures for the protection of coastal and river waters against pollution by nitrates used in agriculture and in municipal waste disposal units, for the treating of used water in urban areas, against the dumping of waste into the sea.

Together with these legal measures, a whole information exchange network is now functioning within the Community, allowing a general keeping of tabs on the level of water pollution and on measures being taken (or not) on a national or local level to combat this pollution.

Finally, as stated earlier, specific programmes like Envireg and Medspa have been set up and are actually functioning and beginning to get results.

Air. There again, a certain number of Community directives have set quality standards and also utilization limits for specific problems such as pollution through lead, sulphur dioxide and suspended particles. Since the acid rain disaster began, measures against pollution by vehicle exhaust fumes have been considerably strengthened (see pages 10 and 86). The Community has also adopted a directive intensifying the struggle against industrial air pollution – in particular through certain types of combustion, of waste incineration and burning of used oil.

The Twelve have also agreed on air quality standards in the use of nitrogen dioxide and on preventive measures against pollution by asbestos.

Noise. The Community has concentrated its attention mainly on noise produced by motor vehicles on the roads, in the air, or on our lawns.

Noise standards have been established and, to take just one example, motorbikes are allowed a 'sound barrier' of 75 decibels if they have 80 cc engines. Since 1990, these standards apply not only to vehicles as a whole, but to spare parts – whether made in or imported into the Community. So, anybody driving around in or on a vehicle that does not conform to Community norms (as proved by the letter E stamped on the appropriate bits) is liable to a fine or to having his vehicle confiscated.

And how can one resist giving this vital piece of information to a nation of gardeners: since 1991, anyone owning or using a lawn-mower more than 120 cm wide (i.e. that cuts a swathe wider than 120 cm) cannot make a noise louder than 90 decibels. So start measuring . . . both your lawn-mower and the noise it makes!

Finally, the noise made by building tools and materials such as pneumatic drills, excavators, cranes, etc. is, little by little, being subjected to maximum nuisance levels agreed on throughout the Community.

Programming better waste disposal units and 'clean' technology

Every year, the Community produces more than 2 billion tons of waste, of which some 30 million tons are considered as dangerous. Around 80% of the waste could come in useful one way or another: by becoming a source of energy, by being recycled, by yielding certain raw materials, etc.

Since 1973, several directives have aimed at better management in the use of waste material. They stipulate that the member States designate a competent authority in charge of waste management, who must draw up plans for the elimination and surveillance of waste material.

Eliminating waste has become a major subject for debate in the various Community countries, especially when it comes to industrial waste. People are not at all keen to see waste disposal units spring up under their noses; somebody, however, has to dispose of this waste, so the existing installations end up by treating waste from all over the place, a system that quite obviously has its limits. France, for instance, annually treats thousands of tons of waste coming from other EC countries, including nuclear waste.

Since 1973, several EC directives have led to: a) the creating in each country of relevant agencies in charge of the surveillance of waste elimination or recycling, b) stricter surveillance of industrial plants who produce, transport or treat toxic waste (1978), c) a very strict control of waste transferrals between countries, especially a number of dangerous waste materials (1981). Not only must the country who is at the receiving end be given very detailed information on the nature of the waste and methods of eliminating it, but so must the relevant EC authorities. The vehicles as well as the route being used to transport the stuff must be clearly described. At the other end, its arrival and the quantity received must be officially notified.

Finally, since the Seveso affair, a 1982 directive has led to the classification of all plants producing toxic material (chemicals, petroleum substances, gas, etc.). Several thousand of them have been classified as dangerous and are therefore the object of particularly strict controls.

Ensuring better nuclear safety

The Chernobyl disaster and the disorderly agitation that ensued have nonetheless had positive results at a Community level. In September 1986, five months after Chernobyl, the Twelve signed the Vienna Convention by virtue of which they pledged themselves to notify the rest of the world immediately in case of a nuclear accident (or simply an abnormal situation) in their respective territories, or on anyone else's when detected.

As for the Community itself, it also took a certain number of initiatives: reinforcing sanitary protection of food against possible contamination, improving information networks in cases of radiological emergencies, installing protection and mutual aid networks in case of accidents or emergency situations, preparing means of informing the public.

Finally, whether it concerns nuclear issues or any other environmental problem, the Community is also intent on developing scientific research so as to take a positive and active part in the fight to protect our environment.

This action is based on a specific programme, called **STEP** (Science and Technology for Environment and Protection). A lot of research is carried out in common by laboratories in the various EC countries as well as in the Community labs. This research concerns the protection of the environment through reducing pollution and pollutants, but also covers nuclear security, technological risks, natural and climatological disasters, and the use of space detection.

But, although the Community is making great efforts, it cannot go very far without its major weapon and incentive: public opinion. Since 1987 was proclaimed European Year of the Environment, and a number of initiatives were taken to inform people on environmental issues, the citizens of the Community have taken a steadily increasing interest in such matters. The Commission also organized a pilot project to encourage the introduction of environmental studies in primary and secondary school curricula.

On top of which, the Community gives financial help and technical assistance to the European Bureau of the Environment, a pressure group settled in Brussels, that represents more than a hundred ecological organizations throughout Europe.

European citizens are encouraged to denounce attacks against the environment. The European Commission receives an ever-increasing number of complaints from individuals, groups, local authorites, etc. against initiatives or organizations that are considered as acting against the environment. Just as an example, in 1984, the Commission received exactly eleven such complaints; by the end of the decade, they had grown to some 450 a year. And that, surely, is far from reflecting reality . . .

7 It all boils down to blackcurrant liqueur

Consumer protection in the European Community is currently at the same stage as environmental matters were fifteen years ago. A rather glum statement from Karel Van Miert, but he should know – he's the European Commissioner in charge of consumer problems. To us humble European consumers it may appear, on the face of it, a rather harsh judgement, especially when we take a look at our supermarket shelves or our shop windows.

Fifteen years ago, we would have been hard put to find Greek yogurt, Italian shoes, Spanish grapes, French apples or German washing-machines (or Italian washing-machines, French yogurt, Greek apples, etc.) at the drop of a hat or, more specifically, at the drop of a few banknotes. We may have been able to find them, but not necessarily at affordable prices. So, surely, greater freedom of trade and circulation has to be a good thing for consumers? It certainly affords them greater choice. The question is whether it affords them better quality for better prices.

Another, vital, question is whether it affords them better information. Uninformed Europeans, be they citizens or consumers, can, after all, be manipulated into accepting products, services and even policies that are not up to standard. And, as you cannot fool all of the people all of the time, this kind of situation usually ends up with everybody getting so wary of being conned that they will stick to their own familiar products or services and will have nothing to do with anything new – which is generally not the best way to promote and develop economic activity.

That, in any case, is the opinion of the EC authorities. They consider that the best way to protect consumers is to treat them like intelligent adults and give them, as much as possible, the means to protect themselves thanks to a few common groundrules and a great deal of practical information. The rules may be few, but they are very important because they set out the basic standards of quality, security and health which must be the same throughout the Community and which every EC consumer should be able to count on, wherever he lives.

THE BATTLE OF
THE BLACKCURRANT

The problem for consumers is that, when the European Common Market was created, the operative word was *Market*, and its main objective since has been to facilitate and develop trade. So practically all the effort was put into encouraging and helping the people responsible for producing and for selling, rather than those who are at the receiving end, namely the buyers. Nowhere in the Treaty of Rome is consumer protection really mentioned and even the Single Act makes no specific reference to the problem, even though, by 1986, when it was drafted, the subject had become very topical. A rather surprising omission, considering that 'consumer-conscious' countries like Denmark and the United Kingdom had joined the Community and might have been expected to insist on this problem being brought up and made the subject of particular clauses.

Actually, quite the reverse happened; according to some nasty suspicious observers of Community lore, Denmark and the UK, to name but those two, soon realized that it was in their own commercial interest to maintain the status quo. Their own stricter consumer laws allowed them to channel and control the influx of Continental goods while taking advantage of slacker consumer protection elsewhere.

A typical example was the French poultry incident, in the early 'eighties. When the French started making inroads into the British market thanks to new ways of presenting and packaging turkey, the British government, under pressure from the farming lobby, suddenly decreed that French poultry was not up to national hygiene standards and forbade its import. This was naturally accompanied by a massive press campaign against that particular French product. The French government appealed to the European Community and, a few months later, the British market was once again opened to poultry from France – but by then, of course, British producers and traders had caught up with the new trend and had got themselves a head start. Where the interest of the consumers was to be found in all this remains a mystery . . .

It is this kind of protectionist strategy that the Community wishes to eliminate once and for all. In that particular instance, the people the Community would like to have seen protected were not so much the French poultry-farmers – who had after all other European markets at their disposal – as the British consumers, who were not consulted or given any choice in the matter.

As it turned out, it was another French food product that brought about a European Court of Justice ruling destined to become just the kind of legal precedent the Commission needed to embark on a practical consumer policy. It happened in 1979; until then the European Community had been beavering away trying to harmonize the various rules and standards on *all* types of goods and services between *all* member States. But it was fighting a losing battle: every time the Commission managed, after months or years of strenuous effort, to harmonize standards for a particular product, one or several member States would immediately evolve another, more stringent, set of national norms for that product, so as to protect their own producers.

In 1976, France appealed to the Court of Justice because it could not export to Germany a product known as *Cassis de Dijon* – a blackcurrant liqueur produced in the Dijon area and which is mixed with white wine to make up a drink called *Kir*, invented, as many alcoholic drinks in France, by a man of God: Chanoine Kir, a famous figure of the French Resistance during the war, also Dijon's Mayor and MP. A man of many parts . . . A German rule forbade the sale of spirits with less than 32% alcoholic content – *Cassis de Dijon* 'only' contained 15 to 20%.

The European Court of Justice took three years to make up its mind (one imagines that a lot of comparative tasting was necessary . . .); in 1979, it decreed that the German regulation amounted to a restriction on foreign imports, in particular alcoholic beverages produced according to the other nation's standards. The Court added a rider to the effect that there was no excuse for refusing entry to alcoholic beverages that were legally and properly produced and sold in another member State, except if these products were recognized as dangerous to human health, or were not being sold in accordance with tax or excise regulations.

There was the opening the Community authorities were looking for. The ruling of the European Court of Justice became the basic criterion for setting the standards of products: if a product, in particular a food product, does not contravene the standards of the country where it is produced, it can be commercialized in any of the other member States.

This ruling was confirmed several times over, when France, Germany and Italy were condemned for imposing their own norms on certain products coming from abroad, namely yogurt, beer and pasta.

COMMUNITY DECISIONS

On the basis of all this, the Community proceeded to elaborate a new approach to the problem of recognizing standards and norms.

1) Since 1984, any new regulation or standard planned by national authorities must, prior to its adoption, be notified to the European Commission, who will inform all the other member States. If necessary, adoption of this new regulation will be suspended until the necessary measures can be taken on a European level to avoid it becoming an obstacle to free trade.

2) Instead of concerning every single product, European directives can be limited to defining basic standards of health and security to which *all* products or services have to conform before being offered throughout the Community.

These basic directives are vital; giving consumers a greater choice is obviously a very positive and important move, but giving them, at the same time, greater protection and security is just as important, if not more.

Many directives have been adopted in several different areas of consumer interest.

Foodstuffs
Rules have been set on presentation and labelling. We are by now all familiar with the kind of information we can be sure of finding on food packaging (ingredients, quantity, time limit for consumption, etc.).

The kind of packaging materials that are directly in contact with the food has also been subjected to rules. Biological and dietary products, including baby food, have also been set quality standards, in particular when it comes to labelling. Since 1992, they must all come with precise explanations on their contents and manufacturing methods. This also concerns fresh meat.

Incubated eggs cannot be sold for eating purposes.

Cattle can no longer be fattened with hormones; in fact, meat containing hormones cannot be imported into the EC (much to the annoyance of American breeders).

Additives, such as dyes or preservatives, can only be used if they figure on a list of accepted products.

Fruit juices, tinned milk, cocoa and chocolate products, coffee extracts, mineral waters, jams, honey and all sorts of other foodstuffs are subject to precise rules governing their different components, their manufacturing and their trade names.

Cosmetics

An EC directive sets the rules for the manufacturing, the packaging and the labelling of cosmetics, suntan lotions, etc. It forbids the use of substances considered as dangerous to people's health, and subjects others, such as dyes, to stringent conditions and restrictions.

Textiles

Their denomination, labelling and fabric control are also subject to several European directives. The use of TRIS, a fire-proof substance which can turn out to be dangerous to people's health, has been forbidden for certain types of clothes.

Dangerous substances

There again, a certain number of directives govern such things as classification, evaluation tests, marketing, labelling and use of substances such as pesticides, solvents, paint, glue, etc.

Pharmaceutical products

Measures taken at EC level are specifically concerned with clinical tests, marketing methods, protection against counterfeits, labelling, and the rights of innovators. One directive in particular makes sure that there is total openness on the question of prices and of National Health reimbursement for medical products.

Another directive extends the quality and security rules governing medicines to vaccines, blood by-products and exports to the Third World – sending our surplus drugs to poorer countries is a good idea, provided manufacturers don't just dump on them medicines that, in our own countries, have been taken off the market because they can have secondary effects. In the past, this has been known to happen.

Manufactured goods

Since 1990, an EC directive has set specific safety and health norms for toys, whether they are made in the Community or imported from elsewhere. These norms are aimed at protecting the Community's 64 million children under fourteen from toys that can be a hazard to health – by poisoning, for instance; or security – such as toys that can be swallowed by small children. Other directives concern greater safety measures in the making of cars and tractors.

Finally, a directive that is still in the making but is expected to have positive effects will make it compulsory for manufacturers and distributors, *in general*, to market products that have been officially declared safe, and only those; member States will also be obliged to make sure that this rule is being applied by keeping watch over their own markets and, when necessary, restricting or forbidding the sale of dangerous products.

INFORMATION AND CONSUMERS' RIGHTS

Another Community objective is maximum information, not only for its 340 million citizens, but for the authorities in each member State. This is already under way thanks to an information network which enables one country to warn the European Commission and all the other member States of any serious incident caused by a consumer product of any nature whatsoever. This enables the various national and European authorities to take the necessary measures to ensure the protection of their citizens – by informing them through the press, for instance, or by forbidding the entry of that product in their territory.

Another network, known as EHLASS (see page 79),

conveys all information concerning accidents in the home and in the course of leisure activities, if they are caused by a particular product or implement.

All this activity is managed by a specific consumer department within the European Commission, under the authority of a Commissioner: namely, at the present time, Karel Van Miert. Linked to this department is a committee, known as the CCC (Consumers Consultative Committee): it unites experts from four consumer organizations – the European Bureau of Consumer Unions, the Committee of Family Organizations, Eurocoop (European Community of Consumer Cooperatives) and the European Trade Union Confederation. In 1989, this Consultative Committee was enlarged to include representatives from national consumers' organizations and turned from Committee into Council. Unfortunately, whether committee or council, it appears that, for the moment, it is not as efficient as it could be, due to a certain lack of unity amongst its members. According to some observers, this is not surprising, as the various organizations, by their very nature, do not always have the same objectives and the same vision – some are more geared to social problems, others are interested in practical consumer questions. It does however have at least the advantage of existing and working.

Making sure that European consumers are being offered a satisfying standard of products is but one aspect of consumer protection. The Community is also keen to protect the public against unlawful or simply rash commercial practices.

Publicity is one of the more visible aspects of commercial activity and, as such, was bound to come under Community scrutiny. The rulings on publicity for tobacco we already know about (see page 78), but there are many European directives covering such questions as misleading publicity, door to door sales, responsibility for damages caused by a defective product, etc.

All these directives have led to the establishment of a common European nexus of guarantees that protect the consumer whatever the country where he has taken his custom. This means that the EC consumer has the right to take legal action against an advertiser for, say, misleading publicity, and it is up to the advertiser to prove that his assertions were truthful.

The EC consumer is entitled to a seven-day period of

consideration during which time he can think over or even cancel a contract if it was signed away from the vendor's place of work – at the client's home, for instance. He is entitled to compensation for any damage caused by a defective product, even if the salesman was not at fault. He is entitled to trustworthy information on the conditions of any payment by instalments, as well as a certain amount of guarantees concerning publicity, advance payments, possible retrieval of goods and conditions of eventual claims against the vendor.

Pre-paid travel and holidays are another area where the public can be very vulnerable in case of dishonest dealings. A directive was adopted in 1990, increasing the responsibility of the professionals who organize and sell pre-paid trips and subjecting them to common rules on such questions as informing their clients and, when necessary, giving them compensation.

The European Commission has also published a recommendation (not a directive) on the issuing of credit cards. Banks have been asked to limit the responsibility of the client in case of loss, theft or counterfeit.

THE LIMITS TO CONSUMER PROTECTION

When all is said and done, there remains a vital question: if the average consumer has all these rights and all this protection, how can he actually use them to defend himself? What courts can he appeal to? What legal help can he obtain? The plain and simple answer is that there isn't much he can do, at least not on his own. Which explains in part why Karel Van Miert considers there is still a lot of work to be done. There is no denying that, in the balance of power as it now exists, the individual consumer is at a distinct disadvantage in an eventual confrontation with the world of production and trade. And in some EC countries, where consumer groups are less well established and well organized, the disadvantage becomes even more glaring.

This is also due to the fact that individuals cannot appeal directly to the European Court of Justice, but must start by going through the legal system of their own country (see page 168); it is only once that is done, and under certain very precise legal conditions, that the case can be brought to the European Court. In certain cases, the European Court of First Instance can be appealed to, particularly when damages are involved. But all this takes time – sometimes several years – and can be expensive so, as individuals, our best resort remains whatever national consumer watchdog body we feel is the most efficient. Consumer protection groups have no excuse for not knowing what action can or cannot be taken at a Community level.

The European Commission cannot force national governments to change their legislation in favour of consumers – it can only ask them to, and, sometimes, this request meets with success. But the Commission cannot go much further without being accused of meddling in a country's interior affairs – an accusation already levelled at every turn by the various governments, when it fits into their scheme of things.

This does not mean, however, that the Community is paralysed. It can, and should, do more – and it might move a bit quicker if public opinion put some pressure on it. It could, for instance, organize a better information network, not only between national authorities, as it already does, but between all the national consumer groups with similar preoccupations. It has also been suggested, as a practical measure, that a consumer protection group in one country should be allowed to take up a complaint issued from another country. In other words, if a British national, for instance, takes action in Britain against a Dutch manufacturer, his complaint could be taken up and used by a Dutch consumer organization to also take action, on a national or a European level, against that manufacturer. We are far from having reached that stage, however. Perhaps, in fifteen years' time . . .

What the European Commission can and does do, is try to carry consumer awareness into schools. Since 1986, it supports exchange programmes between teachers interested specifically in increasing their knowledge of consumer habits and problems throughout the Community. The Commission has also put together, for schools, an information pack on security, entitled 'Safety Pack'.

Finally, the Commission adopted, in 1990, a three-year action programme, with four main objectives.

1) Give consumers more say by:
– increasing the role of the CCC, thanks, in particular, to a

systematic exchange of experiences and information on consumer policies in each member State;
– supporting consumer groups through technical and financial help, especially in the less prosperous areas of the Community;
– encouraging exchanges between producers and consumers.

2) Give consumers more information and make it more appropriate by:
– developing information services through local initiatives, pilot centres, exchange of information material between schools and consumer groups, etc.;
– promoting a policy of openness and helping, through legal measures, consumers to choose in all fairness, especially in such areas as banking and insurance and also by developing the concept of 'quality label' for the best products;
– allowing better means of comparison by publishing the results of comparative studies done by consumer groups and promoting comparative publicity (still forbidden in some member States).

3) Reinforce and guarantee consumer security by:
– taking into account technological evolution and promoting efficient reactions in emergency situations (nuclear incidents, for example);
– extending responsibility for bodily damages to the services sector; modifying still further cosmetic legislation.

4) Promote the right of any EC citizen to buy the product he wishes in the EC country he wishes, at the best price, without being penalized for this when he goes back to his own country by having extra tax slapped on to it the minute he sets foot there.

This also means protecting the consumer against complicated foreign contracts by harmonizing and simplifying trans-border contracts, guarantees and after-sales services.

CONSUMER CULTURE – TOMORROW'S TV TODAY

Question: should culture be treated as a consumer product? No, is Jacques Delors' answer. The President of the European Commission stated his position very clearly during a speech in Paris on 2 October 1989. 'We cannot', he said, 'treat culture in the same way as refrigerators or motorcars.'

All well and good, but this statement begs a second question: is the European Community geared to implement a cultural policy when, after all, refrigerators and motorcars and the like happen to be its main reason for existing? If culture were still based only on the written page or score, the answer would probably be No. But today's culture is mainly that of the spoken word, through radio, and of the moving image, through cinema and television; and what's left of the written word is often printed by a computer and sent by fax. So today's culture would not get very far without technology, and an extremely sophisticated technology at that; we are therefore back to consumer products, *slightly* more complicated than refrigerators and motorcars, but still compatible with the objectives and the means of the European Community institutions.

On top of which, all this technology means that the very concept of national borders is being swept overboard before our very eyes – what with satellites, cable, video today, high definition or digital TV tomorrow (actually more like tea-time today . . .), never mind the practically hourly progress in telecommunications, the European consumer is threatened with a technological, commercial and linguistic tower of Babel; the result might well be chaos throughout Europe, to the extent that the only possible outcome would be to drop everything and let Japanese and American technology take over permanently.

This problem has been exercising the European Commission for nearly ten years – it is well aware that it can only, for the moment, act significantly on the commercial and technical aspects of European culture; but, if it manages to bring some sort of order and cohesion to the audiovisual market, it will already have taken a decisive step towards safeguarding the specific cultures of the Community, if only by making their promotion less expensive. But it has to act with a great deal of caution; regulating technological exchanges in the very sensitive world of media or entertainment does automatically have an effect on cultural exchanges; the problem has already cropped up with the first tentative measures taken by the Community and, as Jacques Delors pointed out, any technical measure in such a controversial field is bound to have far-reaching consequences on the cultural identity of the peoples of Europe. So they'd better be positive . . .

The story so far . . .

On average, 95% of homes in the EC are equipped with a television set. It goes from 77% in Luxembourg where, apparently, they sometimes have better things to do than watch the box, to 99% in Italy, where apparently they don't; in the United Kingdom, for those who are interested, the average is 98%. About 68% of TV programmes broadcast in the EC are of European origin, but that means that the Europeans watch a lot of home-grown productions, not that they watch those made in another EC country. American productions represent more or less a third of programmes shown on European televisions. Those American TV programmes bought by European channels add up to 40% of the world market, whereas less than 10% of international transactions are made up of exchanges between European countries. Simultaneously, the development of satellite and cable television and the advent of high definition television are causing a great deal of expensive technological investment, which no European country on its own can afford to keep up for very long. For satellite TV alone, there are 33 different programmes distributed in Europe (and not only in the EC), coordinated by Eutelsat, an organization representing the national Post and Telecommunications ministries or companies, in particular when it comes to giving out frequencies. By 1994, there should be, over our heads, some 17 TV satellites launched by the Europeans (there are already more than a dozen right now), some by one country alone, some by a group of countries. Competition between channels using different satellites means that, in the same country, viewers will need, or already need, different types of equipment if they want to pick up all the channels. Like, for instance, having several satellite dishes dotted about their garden like plaster gnomes. Few individual customers are quite happy at the idea of going to that kind of expense and inconvenience, so, unless they can latch on to a cable network or some form of collective receiving system, there are not going to be enough viewers per country to bring expenses down. Financial common sense, if nothing else, is therefore causing investors to think in terms of pan-European broadcasting.

All this is being examined with a lot of attention by European Community authorities, with the idea of bringing some sort of coherence to a rather complex situation. The need for overall coherent action was stressed in a Green Paper published by the European Commission in 1984. It was based on a 1983 preliminary report pointing out the need to set up some sort of legal structure to ensure that television programmes would have the same freedom of circulation within the EC as any other form of merchandise. European merchandise, that is . . .

The Green Paper was followed by a Commission directive adopted, after much bickering, in October 1989, under the title 'Television without Frontiers'. Its two basic principles are, on the one hand, freedom of circulation of TV programmes in the EC, on the other, a degree of protection for TV programmes made in Europe.

The directive makes it compulsory for each member State to allow TV programmes from the other member States to be broadcast on its territory. The only restriction concerns programmes that could have an adverse effect on minors.

What about publicity during programmes? That was also regulated, so as to avoid programmes being cut up any old how by the different TV channels. Films and telefilms can only be interrupted for advertisements at the end of 45 minutes; as the average film lasts an hour and a half, that means a single publicity cut. For the rest, ads can only be broadcast in between programmes, unless the programme lasts more than half an hour. On the whole, advertisements must not take up more than 20% of an hour-long broadcast, i.e. 12 minutes in every 60 minutes broadcast. Nor can they take up more than 15% of total daily broadcasts.

The second principle stated by the directive caused the most terrific rumpus amongst European TV authorities. In order to protect and promote European production, the member States are required 'whenever possible' to reserve more than 50% of their broadcasting time for programmes made in Europe. This is minus time given over to newscasts, sports programmes, games, publicity or teletext, so it doesn't actually amount to half a day's broadcast. Nevertheless, several EC countries were unhappy at this clause, which they found much too constricting. As for the Americans, they were furious and, apparently, brought quite a bit of pressure to bear on the European negotiators. Nevertheless, it was adopted thanks to that all-important proviso: 'whenever possible'.

The problem is that, for the moment, we are caught in a somewhat vicious circle. European programmes tend to be expensive because there just aren't enough of them compared to the vast amount churned out across the Atlantic, so TV channels will tend to buy the cheaper programmes from the USA, and who can blame them? But the more American programmes they buy, the fewer chances they give to European productions.

So it was up to the European Community to put its money where its mouth was and help European producers make more programmes. Which it has done, by adopting, in December 1990, a five-year programme known as **Media**, that is financed by a budget of 200 million ECUs (£132 million). Its objective is to stimulate European production and distribution within the European Community, but also encourage its promotion in the USA. Aid goes to TV, but also to cinema production. Media does not give money directly to a particular production, but finances organizations like the European Film Distribution Office (to try and counteract the American hold over distribution) for the international distribution of a particular work; it also finances vocational training programmes, aid to screen-writing or even the translation of a production with the use of subtitles or voice-overs. The money is not a gift; it is an advance on earnings.

The language barrier remains a major problem. If an American TV programme can be sold abroad at an attractive price, it's partly because it has already been sold all over the United States without costing a penny in translations. So Media, together with the European Broadcasting Union and the European Alliance for Television and Culture, has set up a fund, interestingly named **Babel**, to finance the dubbing or subtitling of European programmes in the various languages of the Community. In the first half of 1991, Babel provided these services to some thirty audiovisual productions – films, documentaries, children's programmes, current affairs, etc.

Producing is all very well, but for a production to be successful, it has to be properly marketed. **EuroAim** was therefore created to coordinate and promote the commercial activities of independent producers. Several hundred European production companies now use the services of this organization; the result is a solid audiovisual network, positive contacts and exchanges, and a strong bargaining position for Europeans.

The Media programme is aimed, in part, at helping the smaller Community countries, who do not have the financial or structural means to promote their productions throughout Europe. It is, however, also very useful to the bigger countries. According to Jean Dondelinger, European Commissioner responsible for audiovisual and cultural affairs, the UK is one of the main beneficiaries of the Media programme.

The European Commission is also working on a directive aimed at harmonizing legislation on copyright and royalties. It's a very complex matter, not only because each country has its own system, but because royalties are not limited to books, cinema, radio or television: they now involve data processing and design. All in all, royalties represent something between 3 and 5% of the twelve member States' Gross Domestic Product (*Le Monde*, April 1991).

Finally, one must look to the future, and not such a distant future, either. European TV broadcasting will not be limited to the EC. It already involves countries like Sweden, Norway or Switzerland, to name but a few. So, what we will be looking at is a vast European television space. Therefore the Commission is, as from now, working with the Council of Europe on a project for a cross-border Broadcasting Convention. This Convention will involve not only the twenty-one countries currently members of the Council of Europe, but those East European States that have recently signed a cooperation agreement with the Council. Just wait until they start getting *Coronation Street* in Albania . . .

What they will be getting as from 1993 is **Euronews**, the European equivalent of CNN – the round-the-clock news channel. Based in Lyon, Euronews will be broadcast in five languages (English, French, German, Italian and Spanish) by Eutelsat over the whole of eastern, central and western Europe. It is being financed partly by 13 non-commercial TV channels and partly by Community funds.

BONE MARROW TRANSPLANTS –
THE EUROPEAN CONNECTION

Since November 1991, 300,000 potential bone marrow donors in eight European countries are linked by a common network. The European Donor Secretariat (EDS) was officially inaugurated on 19 November after several years spent slowly but surely coordinating and computerizing the files of the various countries. The first two countries to put their files in common were France and Belgium in 1989, followed by Germany, the UK, the Netherlands, Italy, Spain and Switzerland. Austria and the Scandinavian countries are expected to latch on very soon.

Thanks to this European computer network, financed by the EC, the chances of a patient finding the appropriate donor have been greatly enhanced – in France for instance, fourteen patients had, by 1991, received bone marrow from donors living in the UK and Germany, while fifty-eight French donors had given bone marrow to patients in other Community countries linked to the EDS network.

The medical authorities point out that, after all, a Frenchman may have an Italian grandmother, or a Briton a Dutch great-grandfather, etc., and that genetic links offer a better chance of bone marrow compatibility than national ones.

The
European
Community

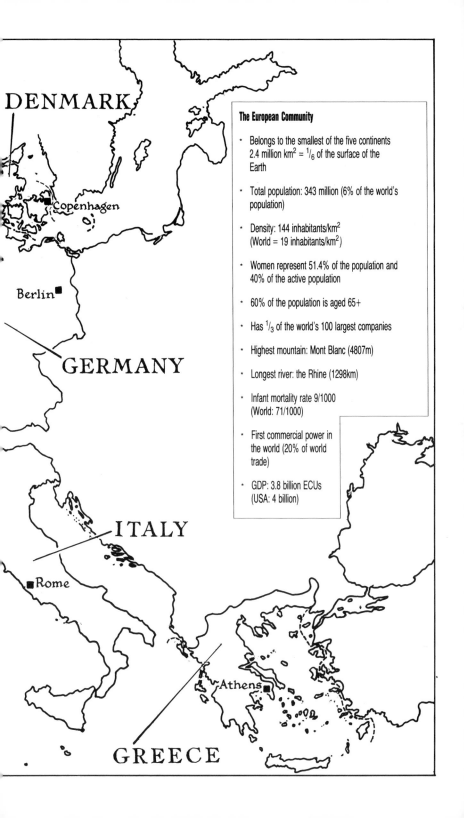

DENMARK

Copenhagen

Berlin

GERMANY

ITALY

Rome

GREECE

Athens

The European Community

* Belongs to the smallest of the five continents
  2.4 million km² = 1/6 of the surface of the
  Earth

* Total population: 343 million (6% of the world's
  population)

* Density: 144 inhabitants/km²
  (World = 19 inhabitants/km²)

* Women represent 51.4% of the population and
  40% of the active population

* 60% of the population is aged 65+

* Has 1/3 of the world's 100 largest companies

* Highest mountain: Mont Blanc (4807m)

* Longest river: the Rhine (1298km)

* Infant mortality rate 9/1000
  (World: 71/1000)

* First commercial power in
  the world (20% of world
  trade)

* GDP: 3.8 billion ECUs
  (USA: 4 billion)

BELGIUM

A cat-lover's paradise.....

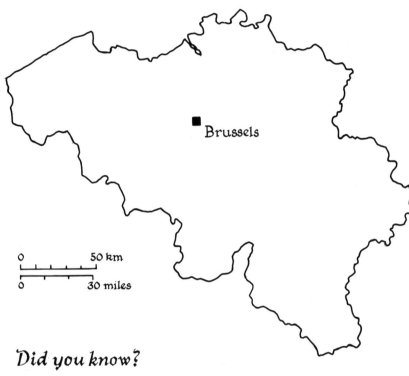

Brussels

0   50 km

0   30 miles

Did you know?

In the European Community, Belgium has:

~ the highest road-accident rate (15 per 1000 vehicles)

~ the highest number of one-parent families (7%)

~ the highest number of young unemployed (45%)

~ the highest number of cat-owners (25% of homes)

~ the widest cable TV network (91% of homes)

Belgium

Capital: Brussels
Total area: 30,500km^2 (1.3% of EC)
Population: 9.9 million (2.9% of EC)
Density: 324 inhabitants/km^2
Languages: French, Dutch
Political system: Constitutional monarchy
Currency: Belgian franc
GDP: 12,800 ECUs/inhabitant

DENMARK

*High incomes,
high taxes.....*

0   80 km

0   50 miles

Copenhagen

Bornholm

Did you know?

In the European Community,
Denmark has:

~ the highest gross
domestic product
(GDP: 17,738 ECUs/inhabitant)

~ the highest income tax
(53% minimum)

~ the highest suicide rate
(26/100,000 inhabitants)

~ the highest divorce rate
(2.9/1000 inhabitants)

Denmark

Capital: Copenhagen
Total area: 43,100km^2 (1.8% of EC)
Population: 5.1 million (1.5% of EC)
Density: 119 inhabitants/km^2
Language: Danish
Political system: Monarchy
Currency: Crown
GDP: 17,738 ECUs/inhabitant

FRANCE

Holiday homes galore.....

Paris

Lyon

200 km

0

100 miles

0

Marseille

Corsica

Did you know?

In the European Community,
France has:

~ the largest total area (549,000 km²)

~ the greatest amount of forests (27%)

~ the longest holidays
(5-6 weeks a year)

~ the highest ownership of
holiday homes (12% of families)

~ the highest life expectancy
for women (80.7 years)

~ the highest consumption of
medicines (29 per inhabitant/year)

France

Capital: Paris
Total area: 549,000km² (23% of EC)
Population: 56.3 million (16.4% of EC)
Density: 102 inhabitants/km²
Language: French
Political system: Republic
Currency: French franc
GDP: 14,400 ECUs/inhabitant

GERMANY

A car for two.....

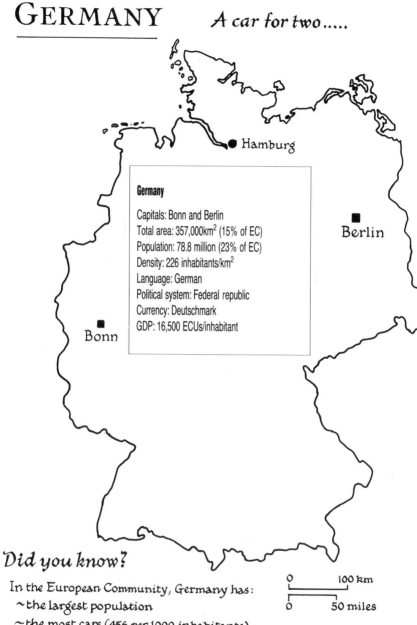

● Hamburg

Germany

Capitals: Bonn and Berlin
Total area: 357,000km^2 (15% of EC)
Population: 78.8 million (23% of EC)
Density: 226 inhabitants/km^2
Language: German
Political system: Federal republic
Currency: Deutschmark
GDP: 16,500 ECUs/inhabitant

■ Berlin

■ Bonn

Did you know?

In the European Community, Germany has:
- ~the largest population
- ~the most cars (456 per 1000 inhabitants)
- ~the greatest number of museums (2025) and public libraries (11,500)
- ~the longest river (the Rhine: 1298 km)
- ~the highest number of accidents at work (13 deaths/100,000 workers)

0   100 km

0   50 miles

GREECE

Boosting the tobacco industry .....

Athens

0   100 km

0   50 miles

Did you know?

In the European Community, Greece has:

- ~ the most sunshine
  (2600 hours/year)

- ~ the greatest number of farmers
  (13.6 of working population)

- ~ the largest defence budget
  (6.6% of GDP)

- ~ the greatest number of smokers
  (43% of the population)

Greece

Capital: Athens
Total area: 132,000km² (5.6% of EC)
Population: 10 million (2.6% of EC)
Density: 76 inhabitants/km²
Language: Greek
Political system: Republic
Currency: Drachma
GDP: 4400 ECUs/inhabitant

IRELAND

It rains dogs....

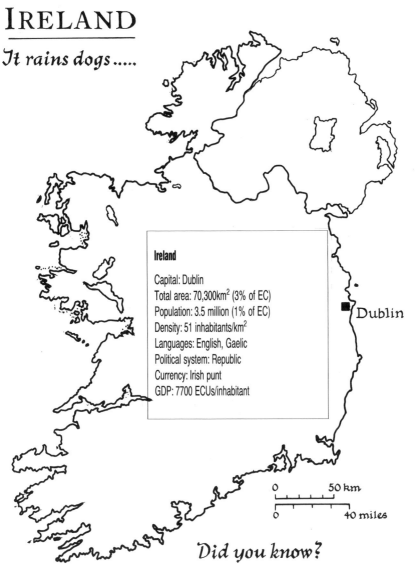

Ireland

Capital: Dublin
Total area: 70,300km^2 (3% of EC)
Population: 3.5 million (1% of EC)
Density: 51 inhabitants/km^2
Languages: English, Gaelic
Political system: Republic
Currency: Irish punt
GDP: 7700 ECUs/inhabitant

Dublin

```
0        50 km
├──┼──┼──┼──┤
0        40 miles
```

Did you know?

In the European Community, Ireland has:

~ the highest birth rate (2.11 children/woman)

~ the lowest marriage rate (5 on a scale of 5 to 7)

~ the highest number of young people (28% under 15)

~ the highest unemployment rate (16.7%)

~ the greatest consumption of potatoes
   (141 kg per inhabitant/year)

~ the highest proportion of dog-owners
   (40% of homes)

ITALY

TV yes, bambini no......

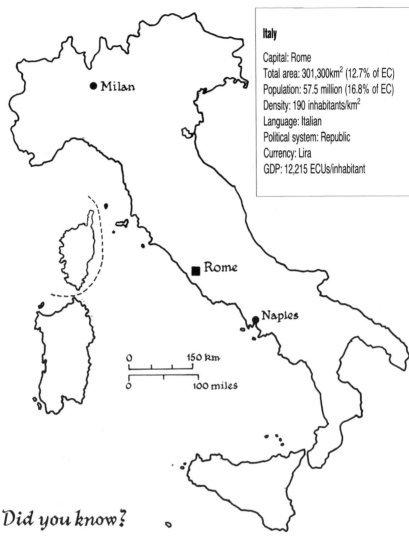

● Milan

Italy

Capital: Rome
Total area: 301,300km^2 (12.7% of EC)
Population: 57.5 million (16.8% of EC)
Density: 190 inhabitants/km^2
Language: Italian
Political system: Republic
Currency: Lira
GDP: 12,215 ECUs/inhabitant

■ Rome

● Naples

0 ——— 150 km

0 ——— 100 miles

Did you know?

In the European Community, Italy has:
~ the greatest rainfall (equal with the UK, 95 cm/year)
~ the lowest birthrate (1.3 children/woman)
~ the highest number of TV set owners (98% of families)
~ the highest number of small businesses

LUXEMBOURG

Home of the happy European.....

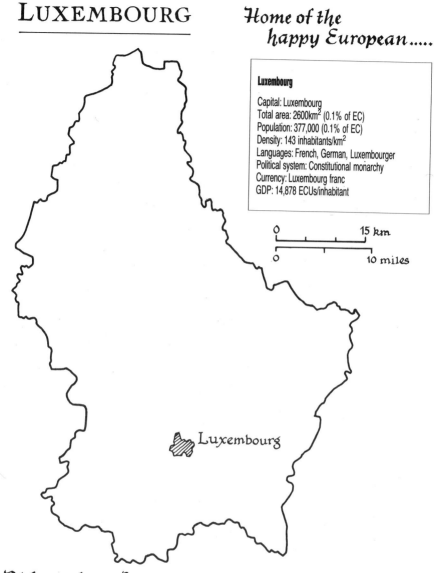

Luxembourg

Capital: Luxembourg
Total area: 2600km^2 (0.1% of EC)
Population: 377,000 (0.1% of EC)
Density: 143 inhabitants/km^2
Languages: French, German, Luxembourger
Political system: Constitutional monarchy
Currency: Luxembourg franc
GDP: 14,878 ECUs/inhabitant

Luxembourg

Did you know?

In the European Community, Luxembourg has:
- ~ the highest level of carbon monoxide (6.5 t per inhabitant/year)
- ~ the highest proportion of foreigners (25% of population)
- ~ the highest number of house owners (81% of homes)
- ~ the highest ownership of washing machines (97% of homes) and dishwashers (98% of homes)
- ~ the highest proportion of satisfied citizens (97%)

THE NETHERLANDS

Keeping up the Community spirit.....

0   50 km

0   25 miles

Amsterdam ■

■ The Hague

● Rotterdam

Did you know?

In the European Community,
the Netherlands has:

~ the highest population density
(356 inhabitants/km²)

~ the highest number of boats
(27/1000 inhabitants)

~ the highest life expectancy
for men (73.7 years)

~ the highest number of
compact discs
(60 per 1000 inhabitants)

~ the highest proportion of
pro-Europeans (84%)

The Netherlands

Capitals: Amsterdam, The Hague
Total area: 41,785km² (1.8% of EC)
Population: 14.8 million (4.3% of EC)
Density: 356 inhabitants/km²
Language: Dutch
Political system: Monarchy
Currency: Florin
GDP: 13,094 ECUs/inhabitant

PORTUGAL

The shortest school terms.....

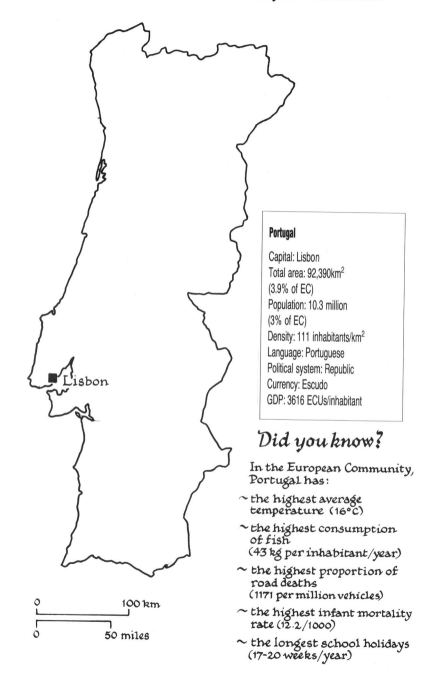

Portugal

Capital: Lisbon
Total area: 92,390km^2
(3.9% of EC)
Population: 10.3 million
(3% of EC)
Density: 111 inhabitants/km^2
Language: Portuguese
Political system: Republic
Currency: Escudo
GDP: 3616 ECUs/inhabitant

Did you know?

In the European Community, Portugal has:

~ the highest average temperature (16°C)

~ the highest consumption of fish
(43 kg per inhabitant/year)

~ the highest proportion of road deaths
(1171 per million vehicles)

~ the highest infant mortality rate (12.2/1000)

~ the longest school holidays
(17-20 weeks/year)

Lisbon

0   100 km

0   50 miles

SPAIN

The rain falls mainly elsewhere .....

Barcelona

Madrid

0   200 km

0   100 miles

Did you know?

In the European Community, Spain has:

~ the biggest fleet (2350 ships)

~ the greatest number of doctors (338/100,000 inhabitants)

~ the greatest number of temporary workers (22% of workers)

~ the sunniest climate (with Greece), the hottest temperatures (with Portugal)

Spain

Capital: Madrid
Total area: 504,800km^2 (21.3% of EC)
Population: 38.9 million (11.3% of EC)
Density: 77 inhabitants/km^2
Languages: Spanish, Catalan
Political system: Parliamentary monarchy
Currency: Peseta
GDP: 7383 ECUs/inhabitant

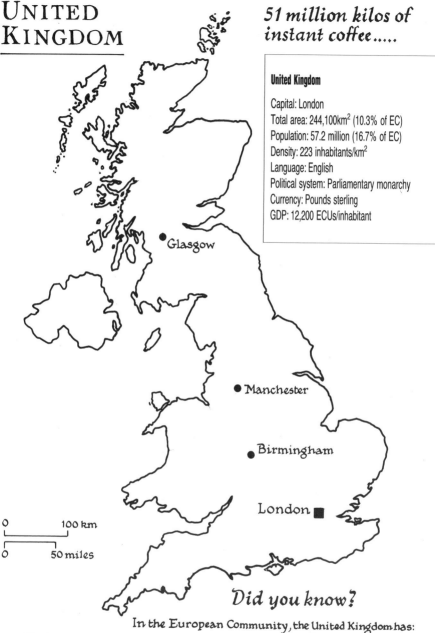

UNITED KINGDOM

51 million kilos of instant coffee.....

United Kingdom

Capital: London
Total area: 244,100km^2 (10.3% of EC)
Population: 57.2 million (16.7% of EC)
Density: 223 inhabitants/km^2
Language: English
Political system: Parliamentary monarchy
Currency: Pounds sterling
GDP: 12,200 ECUs/inhabitant

● Glasgow

● Manchester

● Birmingham

London ■

0 —— 100 km
0 —— 50 miles

Did you know?

In the European Community, the United Kingdom has:

~ the largest amount of money spent on publicity (1.6% of GDP)
~ the greatest number of scientific Nobel Prizes (63)
~ the widest use of contraception (83% of couples)
~ the highest number of cassette tapes (131 per inhabitant)
~ the highest consumption of instant coffee (0.9 kg per inhabitant/year)

FAMOUS LAST WORDS . . .

When European negotiations are enlivened by the British going around saying 'no' to everything, the other negotiators rarely fly into a panic – it's more a 'here we go again' kind of reaction and people tend to reminisce about all the times the UK started off by digging in its heels and then, eventually, let itself be persuaded into joining the gang.

The UK's first – and most famous – 'no' came when it was asked to join the group of countries preparing the 1957 Treaty of Rome. The scene has remained vivid in the minds of those who were present at the preparatory talks, where London had sent a representative. After days of total silence, the British delegate suddenly got up and said: 'Gentlemen, I have listened to your discussions with interest and sympathy. I must tell you that this future treaty you have been asked to prepare is not likely to be concluded; should it be concluded, it's not likely to be ratified; should it be ratified, it's even less likely to be applied.' And he left the talks.

Sixteen years later, the United Kingdom signed the Treaty. Not before finding itself at the receiving end of a refusal, however. When the British first applied, in 1963, it was General de Gaulle, President of France, who answered: 'Non!'

The British were not amused.

8 The master plan

A PRACTICAL CONCEPT – 1950-58

Rome, we are always being told, wasn't built in a day; so, with hindsight, it was certainly the most appropriate place to choose when it came to laying the first foundation stone of the European Community. That was thirty-five years ago, and the Community is still at the building stage even if, like the London Docklands, a lot of it is habitable and many people live there most comfortably.

In any case, the Treaty of Rome, signed in 1957, turned out to be a very sturdy foundation stone, carved out of strong material – to whit, an intelligent, practical and flexible concept.

The idea of uniting Europe one way or another – usually with the help of an army or two – often occurred in the past to various historical figures, starting aptly enough with a man who did his bit towards building Rome, namely Julius Caesar; but it took the appalling shock of the Second World War for some European political leaders to take a step back for a better appraisal of the situation and assert that the people of Europe must surely have better things to do than go for each other's throats on a regular basis. And, what is more, they actually meant what they said. The problem was to go from meaning it to actually doing something about it, with the consent of a group of nations who, at that particular time, were not overwhelmed by brotherly feelings for one another. Yet everybody was aware that the time had come to put aside nationalistic attitudes, those very attitudes that had been responsible for the war in the first place. That was as good a starting point as any. A second one was the desire to ensure for Europe, or what remained of a free Europe after the Yalta carve-up, a democracy as strong as that of the United States, so that dictatorship would have a very hard time rearing its ugly head again on European soil.

Having said that, no single country was prepared to relinquish its national sovereignity – if only because it just did not trust its neighbours. This didn't stop ten countries from setting up the Council of Europe in Strasbourg in 1949, but the Council had no executive powers, only consultative ones, except in one particular field, that of Human Rights. The Human Rights Court can be appealed to by any individual from one of the twenty-one countries now members of the Council (except Turkey, Cyprus and Malta), and its rulings supersede those of national courts (remember the caning in schools controversy?).

It was obvious that there were just too many European nations with too many diverging interests to be able to get any sort of political system off the ground and in working order. Everybody had more or less reached a stalemate when on 9 May 1950, the French Minister for Foreign Affairs, Robert Schuman, came up with a proposal that turned out, eventually, to be the right plan for designing the European Community.

The original idea didn't belong to Schuman, but to another Frenchman, Jean Monnet, a brilliant economist and financial consultant to major politicians. (The story of the EC seems to be dotted about with Frenchmen, so gird your loins and bear with me!) Monnet was convinced that the only way to unite Europe was, firstly, to start on a relatively modest scale, with just a fistful of countries, and, secondly, to get these countries together on just one or two initial points of common industrial or economic interest. He put this idea to Robert Schuman, who not only approved of it, but had the political clout to carry it through.

Europe, argued Monnet and Schuman, musn't be perceived as one vast box, where everybody and everything has to be fitted willy-nilly; it's like a house, with many different rooms that are joined by one or more common partitions and doors that can be sometimes open, sometimes shut, but must never be locked; one of these funny old houses where the rooms have been built on at different times, not necessarily in the same style or the same size, but which end up with an attractiveness and a lived-in look all of their own.

What both men suggested, as a starting point, was to place French and German production of coal and steel under the responsibility of a single high authority within an organization that would always be open to any other European nation who wished to join. The advantage of this proposal was to link by a common bond Europe's two worst enemies while avoiding delicate political issues such as recognizing Germany as a sovereign State or not. It was accepted enthusiastically and other countries asked to join; so, on 18 April 1951, the Treaty of Paris instituting the European Coal and Steel Community (ECSC) was signed not by two, but by six countries – Belgium, France, Italy, Luxembourg, the Netherlands and West Germany – those same ones who were to sign the Treaty of Rome six years later. And that's how Jean Monnet earned the distinction of being dubbed 'the Father of Europe'.

The ECSC was an interesting model for the Founding Fathers of the Common Market to work on, not only because of its basic principles, outlined by the Monnet–Schuman team, but also because of the way it was organized. It wasn't simply a free-trading association, where trade barriers between countries are abolished or at least diminished but where it's still each one for himself. In the ECSC, competition between member States when dealing with external markets was governed by a set of rules, so that deals could not be made for the benefit of just one member to the detriment of one, several or all of the others. Each country kept its own steel and coal industry, and was free to do business with the rest of the world, provided this business brought about greater prosperity and economic progress for the ECSC market as a whole. It was, in a sense, a club whose members were bound by a common interest – in this case coal and steel – and, like any other club, it had to have one or several bodies responsible for implementing the rules and regulations, keeping everything in good working order and eventually coming up with ideas and initiatives for adding to the prosperity of the club. The ECSC treaty therefore provided for an elected body to lay down the rules and make the decisions that would then be carried out by an independent executive body, as well as for a judicial body who could be appealed to in case of problems.

The success of the ECSC prompted the six countries to think

about extending the system to cover the whole of the economic spectrum and creating a proper European Economic Community. How? The ECSC and the Jean Monnet 'philosophy' were going to be the basis on which to start building.

It then became a question of deciding how many rooms to start off with, in what order.

In June 1955, the Ministers for Foreign Affairs of the six ECSC countries met in Messina, Sicily, and came up with a text that specified the long-term objectives for an economic community: a united Europe, they said, should be achieved by developing common institutions, progressively blending national economies, creating a common market and harmonizing social policies. At the time, the United Kingdom was asked to join in the discussions, but refused.

The Ministers also established what the conditions for achieving these aims should be:

1) the barriers to free trade exchanges between countries should be progressively removed and identical customs regulations applied towards outside countries;

2) competition between member States should not be allowed to lead to protectionist attitudes or measures by any one member towards the others;

3) a coordinated monetary policy should be implemented where necessary;

4) special aid should be forthcoming for the poorer and less developed areas of the Community;

5) freedom of movement within the Community should be granted to workers beloning to any of the member States;

6) social policies should be progressively coordinated with a view to achieving the same treatment for workers throughout the Community.

So, as far back as 1955, the basic principles of the European Community, and the major conditions for making them work, were already set down. These principles and conditions still represent, today, the goal the Community must achieve if it is to become a solidly united Europe.

Following the Messina meeting, the Belgian Minister for Foreign Affairs, Paul-Henri Spaak, was asked to put all these ideas and principles into some sort of practical shape. In April 1956, he submitted a document known as the Spaak Report, where he spelt out what kind of institutions would be needed to make a 'common market' function properly. He had listed four major ones: a permanent, independent Commission who would come up with ideas and initiatives; a Council made up of representatives of each member State who would take the decisions arising from the proposals of the Commission; a Court of Justice to act as arbitrator and, finally, a Parliament to make sure that democracy and the opinions of citizens would be respected.

The Spaak Report was followed by months of intensive negotiating, in Brussels, with a view to hammering out a proper treaty – a document that would set out, once and for all, the aims, the structures and the rules of the European Community. The difficulty was to put together a project that was flexible, so that no single member would feel it was being hassled into taking measures against its own interests but, at the same time, was strong enough to resist any move towards perverting or even destroying the very nature of the Community. The answer to that problem was to a) set up the various institutions mentioned above, which gave the Community structured protection against national whims and squabbles, b) give the Community a very precise objective that everybody agreed on. And that objective was to, progressively, turn the Community into one common trading zone, with no more inner customs barriers.

On the face of it, this objective looks clear-cut and straightforward. In actual fact, it implies a vast amount of changes in a variety of different fields, including politics. Just to take a case in point, Belgium, France, Italy and the Netherlands had privileged trade links with countries that had been or were still, at the time, their colonies. With a common market, no one member country could keep those special outside links – these had to be renegotiated so that the outside country could trade with each and every one of the EEC nations in exactly the same way; however, those special bilateral links usually meant that the outside country was receiving aid in some form or another. This aid obviously could not be stopped but, instead of being the responsibility of just one member, it was to be dispensed by the EEC as a whole. As a matter of fact, this particular problem in the build-up towards a common market was so glaringly obvious that the Treaty of Rome itself made specific provision for relations between the Community and the colonies or ex-colonies involved.

Another well-known example was that of agriculture. This question was so intricate and fraught with possible disagreements that it threatened to delay any final decision, and discussions would have dragged on for years. So, instead of trying to work a particular clause into the Treaty, like the one on special relations with outside nations, it was decided that agriculture would of course be included but only in very general terms and would be made the object of a separate agreement later on, after the Treaty was signed.

In any case, whatever the problem, nobody imagined for a moment that it could be solved quickly and easily. Every time a decision is made on one important aspect of European economic cooperation, it's like throwing a pebble into a pond – the ripples go out in ever-growing circles until the whole pond is affected.

There is no way the economy of a continent, let alone a country, can be isolated from its political and social evolution. Which is why it was decided that the first and foremost objective of the Treaty, i.e. a common and single trading zone, on which everybody agreed, should take about twelve to fifteen years to achieve, in successive phases of three to four years. In the course of each phase, a carefully calculated number of measures would be taken – they would consist, naturally, of eliminating trade barriers one after the other, but also of solving the legal, social or political problems directly linked to the fall of each barrier.

At this point, the story is interrupted by those anti-marketeers who have bothered to pay attention to the unfolding of the plot: so, they say, from the very start, the aim of the European Community was to go beyond economic unity; it was actually destined to take over all fields of social relationships and activities throughout Europe . . .

Yes, up to a point; but only up to a point. The fabric of society is so tightly knit you can't just pull on one thread and hope that the rest are going to stay put. The men and women involved in conceiving the Treaty of Rome were well aware that they were preparing changes both far-reaching and wide-ranging in the way Europe functioned. They were also aware that they could not decide then what Europe would look like twenty, thirty or forty years later. They therefore stuck to one basic principle: they were going to prepare the ground for one major economic move, which would be to blend European economies into one single market. Every step taken towards this common goal would of course have non-economic side effects calling for non-economic measures.

But these measures, says the Treaty, should be taken only in so far as they are directly and immediately linked to the proper functioning of the European Community. In other words, when pulling out one thread, we will make sure that only those threads nearest to it are affected, and not the whole fabric. It will be decided in due course if and when it is necessary to pull out another thread and then another.

That is what the European institutions are for: it is their job to judge what effect such and such a trade barrier coming down is going to have, whether it's going to affect transport or agriculture, jobs or salaries, justice or communications, and so on. These effects will have to be taken into account and the appropriate measures will have to be taken, either by the Community or by national institutions. Every time, the balance between national and supranational decisions will be carefully observed so that no member State is bullied into accepting measures contrary to its own interests. One plain, vigorous objective – many variable, flexible means of achieving it. It was the very essence of the Treaty of Rome and it's still the way the Community is being handled today. After all, the proof of the pudding is in the eating and, thirty-five years on, nobody has yet come up with a better idea than the text signed in Rome on 25 March 1957, the foundation stone of a European Economic Community, due to start going up officially on 1 January 1958.

Another treaty was signed that day, instituting the European Atomic Energy Community. This organization, known as Euratom, was designed to set up the necessary conditions for creating and developing non-military nuclear industries as well as a common nuclear research network. This Atomic Energy Community has its own symbol in the shape of the Euratom Building or Atomium in Brussels, which bears the aspect of a gigantic molecular structure. The Atomium is visited every year by hundreds of thousands of tourists from all over the world.

STRENGTHENING FOUNDATIONS, WIDENING THE BASE – 1958-72

After the Treaty was signed in Rome, then ratified by the six national Parliaments, there followed ten years of hard work building the framework of the Community. A nine-member European Commission (two Frenchmen, two Germans, two

Italians, one Belgian, one Dutchman, one Luxembourger) was designated for four years to start the ball rolling. It settled in Brussels and started recruiting staff–this was a 'temporary' measure until a 'permanent' European 'capital' was decided on. It is still in the process of being decided.

From the very start, it had been obvious that agricultural problems could not be lumped in with the rest of the economy–there was too much disparity between farming systems within the six member States. At the time, agriculture could not be considered in the same light as industry–it was more a way of life, a social system, that each country was keen to protect. So, well before the Common Market came into existence, all national agricultural policies had included some form of price control for major food products so as to avoid farmers suffering the effects of unstable production and wavering markets. This of course was not at all in the spirit of the Treaty of Rome–but it was impossible, on the one hand, to let the wild winds of free markets batter away at an activity that was still picking itself up after the terrible problems of the war and, on the other hand, to keep out of the Community a vital part of the overall economy. The Six were therefore faced with a problem that had strong social and political, as well as economic, implications. For that reason, although the Treaty of Rome specifically includes the agricultural question by mentioning the need to achieve stable markets, secure supplies, reasonable prices, improved productivity and proper living standards for farmers, it also stresses that these objectives can only be attained through a common agricultural 'policy'. The use of the word 'policy' was a way of recognizing that the problem could not be solved by a few common rules and regulations, but had to be studied in a global political context, and be subjected to a separate overall agreement by the six national authorities.

This agreement was reached in July 1958 at Stresa, in Italy, when the basic principles and objectives of a common policy were laid out. As with all the other Common Market activities, the major aim was freedom to exchange agricultural products between member States. Secondly, the prices of agricultural products would be supported, not by each individual country, but by the Community as a whole; the extent, nature and limits of this support would be determined in the spring of each year. Thirdly, agricultural products within the Community would benefit from a commercial preference: practically, this means that food products imported from outside the Community that are cheaper than the same foodstuffs produced within it are subject to a levy which brings their price on a par with Community prices. At the same time, to encourage exports, producers who sell their food outside the Community benefit from a financial help that allows them to bring down the price of their products and be competitive on world markets.

Having established the principles of a Common Agricultural Policy, the Six then had to agree on the financial means to make it work.

This took a little more time and very strenuous discussions; it was only four years later, in 1962, that a negotiation destined to be the first of many Brussels 'marathons' resulted in the European Fund for Agricultural Orientation and Guarantee being set up. Every European country contributed to this Fund by means of various taxes; this national contribution was not proportionate to the amount the Fund would pay back in agricultural aid: one country who paid in a lot would not necessarily receive a lot; it depended on each country's needs. One of the contributions towards the Fund was by means of a tax on products imported from outside the Common Market. (This explains why, when the UK later joined the Common Market, it found itself paying vast amounts of tax to the Fund, since it imported a great deal from the Commonwealth countries, while getting less aid for its farmers than countries like France or Italy – who had a much larger farming community.)

These measures may have smacked of protectionism but the Common Market was certainly not alone in taking this kind of attitude. The United States were, and are, just as protectionist towards their own farmers, and Switzerland even more so.

Europe in the 'fifties and early 'sixties had a vast farming community, not only in France or Italy, but in West Germany as well, and no country was ready to run the risk of finding itself with an equally vast army of unemployed. Farmers meant votes, and unemployed farmers meant trouble. The outcome of all this was that agriculture, since July 1958, is one area of the European economy where national governments have hardly any room for manoeuvring and the major decisions are taken by the Community, the other area being coal and steel, thanks to the ECSC.

While negotiations on farming were going on, other steps in other fields were being taken.

On 31 December 1961, all restrictions on the amount of industrial goods traded within the boundaries of the Community were abolished.

By 1963, a succession of measures had resulted in customs duties between member States being reduced by 60%.

In 1965, the ECSC, Euratom and the European Economic Community (EEC) or Common Market were grouped under a single identity, that of European Community, or EC.

In 1967, Value Added Tax was introduced: it meant that all goods and services within the Community were submitted to an identical system (if not an identical amount) of commercial tax.

And, just ten and a half years after the Treaty of Rome was signed, on 1 July 1968, the Customs Union was born. This means that customs duties within the EC were abolished (as opposed to excise or indirect taxation, which was not) and a common tariff was applied to outside goods imported into any of the member States. This was a very satisfying achievement, well ahead of schedule – the Customs Union had initially been programmed for 1970 at the earliest!

The Common Market, as everybody insisted, and often still insists, on calling it, was doing well. It was being built, as Jean Monnet had said, stone by stone, measure by measure. The six member countries found their economy progressing in leaps and bounds. Their gross domestic product doubled in fifteen years, their yearly growth rate going up as high as 5%, double that of the United States. Of course, they were starting practically from scratch, and they were benefiting from general economic prosperity prior to the first great petrol crisis of 1973.

But the Common Market played an important part in this increased prosperity: it facilitated the mechanisms of economic growth and was a major incentive towards investing, creating and innovating, not only for European businessmen, bankers and industrialists, but also for American ones, who were vastly encouraged at finding a major outlet and client on the other side of the Atlantic.

During all this time, other European countries were showing a growing interest in the EC. The United Kingdom, Ireland, Denmark and Norway started negotiating their eventual entry into the Community as early as 1961, only three years after the

Treaty of Rome was signed. But these negotiations were halted fifteen months later at the instigation of France, who felt that the various candidates were not really entering into the spirit of the thing but seemed to consider that Community rules had to be changed for their own benefit. After a lot of nasty remarks had been bandied back and forth, everybody calmed down and the four countries renewed their application in 1967. This time no chances were being taken. In December 1969, at The Hague, the Heads of State and leaders of the Six set down the conditions that would have to be accepted by all applicants. These conditions were simply that a nation wanting to join the European Community would have to comply with all the articles of the Treaty of Rome, accept its basic principles and its objectives as well as adopting all the Community measures decided and applied since 1958. These conditions were accepted and negotiations officially opened on 30 June 1970 in Luxembourg. The actual Acts of adhesion were signed in Brussels on 22 January 1972. They were ratified by the British, Danish and Irish Parliaments and the three nations became members of the European Community on 1 January 1973. Norway backed out after a referendum in October 1972 resulted in a majority of hostile votes.

STALEMATE! – 1972–85

No sooner had the UK, Ireland and Denmark joined the European Community than the momentum which had spurred it on seemed to peter out. This was nobody's fault, and everybody's fault. In 1973, the Six Days' War between Egypt and Israel, and the Arab petrol embargo that followed caused a world-wide economic crisis. Europe was not spared, far from it. Some European nations were more severely hit than others by petrol shortages; the luckier ones didn't precisely rush to the help of the others; European solidarity was definitely not the order of the day. Each country took its own brand of measures, automatically resulting in whatever form of protectionism was available.

Meanwhile, the three new member countries were adapting more or less easily to their Community status and obligations. The Republic of Ireland took to the EC like a duck to water – if only because its large farming community quickly reaped the benefits of the European agricultural policy. Denmark was not markedly enthusiastic but, true to their nature, the Danes doggedly applied the common discipline and, without any major fuss, adapted themselves and their economy so as to make the best of Community measures and resources. If anyone was playing Hamlet at that point, it was the UK.

To be or not to be in the EC was apparently the question that disrupted every British politician's slumber. Edward Heath, responsible for Britain's entry into the Community, was ousted by a Labour majority, who immediately demanded a renegotiation of Britain's terms of entry, or else! So, in 1975, the European Council meeting in Dublin adopted a new system of financial contribution for each member State which the British considered to be less prohibitive for themselves. (This was the era of the three-day week, of power strikes and other severe economic problems for Britain.) True to its public anti-European stance during the elections, the Labour government, while not wanting to take the responsibility of actually pulling the country out of the EC, decided to leave the decision to the British people by organizing a referendum. On 5 June 1975, the referendum resulted in a 67.2% vote in favour of staying in the EC. So Britain, willy-nilly, remained; this, to the rest of the Community, came as rather a mixed blessing since, in the years that followed, the British mainly acted as though their chief objective was to slow down the progress of the EC as a whole and they were often accused by the European press of being America's 'moles'.

It would be unjust, however, to lay the blame on Britain for all the problems the Community was facing. A large measure of responsibility lay in the very procedure used when taking major decisions – and even minor ones, come to that. As was stipulated by the Treaty of Rome, it was the European Council of Ministers (where every country is represented by the Minister in charge of the questions being discussed) who took the final decision on the proposals put forward by the European Commission.

The problem was that decisions on major questions had to be taken unanimously; all it needed was for one member to disagree on a detail and the whole discussion fell through – unless, eventually, some sort of compromise could be reached on that particular point. This could mean months of acrimonious squabbles, while public opinion became steadily more convinced that the EC was just one huge gunfight at the OK Corral.

Another problem was that the Council was the only body entitled to take decisions – even the smallest and least important ones. So months could be lost fighting over ridiculous details, while important questions were being held up. A typical – and infamous – story is the one about the quantity of sugar allowed in jam. After various discussions, the Council hammered out an agreement in 1972, but as soon as Britain arrived, the result was jeopardized by the soul-searing question of whether or not British marmalade was to be considered as 'jam'. A definitive agreement was finally reached – in 1988.

All this, however, did not stop the building of the Community from continuing. At the 1969 Heads of State meeting at The Hague, which had spelt out the conditions for any country wishing to join the EC, another important decision was taken, although at the time it attracted less attention than all the kerfuffle about enlargement and new memberships. The various Heads of State and of government agreed that the time had come to launch another phase in the building by working towards a final Economic and Monetary Union – which meant a common monetary system, eventually a common currency. This, however, was anathema to a country like Britain, who clung to its financial independence and did not want to put the Pound on a par with other European currencies it considered as weak and unstable. Germany, who was already Europe's economic leader, was also quite wary – though it approved of the principle – because it also feared that the Deutschmark would suffer from too close a contact with less stable currencies. So, while – nearly – everybody paid lip service to the beautiful idea of Monetary Union, actual practical decisions took a long time coming.

The Community, however, soldiered on. Progress continued, new measures were taken, even though they weren't all spectacular media material, so the people of the EC weren't always made really aware of their importance.

The European Community entered over those years into a series of agreements with outside countries that eventually brought about its recognition as the world's first trading power and, most important, as a single trading partner. Since 1973, it is a member, as the European Community, of GATT (General Agreement on Tariffs and Trade). That same year it established a working relationship with EFTA (European Free Trade Association) grouping Norway, Finland, Sweden, Austria,

Switzerland and Iceland, by abolishing customs duties on industrial products exchanges.

In 1975, the first Lomé* Convention was signed between the EC and forty-six countries from Africa, the Caribbean and the Pacific; under the terms of this agreement, the Community undertook to provide these countries with financial support for development projects in many different fields – agriculture, industry, education, health, water supply and so on. It also undertook to grant free access within its borders to agricultural and manufactured products from these countries. There have been two more Lomé Conventions – the last in 1984, grouping sixty-six countries.

1975 was also the year a new European institution was born. The European 'summits' stopped being a simple meeting of Heads of State and became the European Council, whose chief function is to determine and orientate major policy guidelines.

Finally, in 1975, the European Regional Development Fund was set up to bring aid to specific regions within the Community that were underdeveloped or in economic difficulties.

In 1979, another series of important initiatives were carried out. The parliamentary assembly suggested by the Spaak Report and effectively created by the Treaty of Rome had, in 1962, been given the title of European Parliament. Its 198 members were elected by national parliaments. In 1979, for the very first time, they were elected by direct universal suffrage. The number of Euro-MPs went up to 410 (and 434 when Greece later entered the EC). This new mode of election did not give rise to unbridled enthusiasm amongst European voters. On average, 61% of them took the trouble to actually go and put a name in the ballot-box. Attitudes varied according to countries: in the UK, only 32% of the electorate took part in the vote, against 91% in Belgium and 82% in Italy. Voters would probably have displayed more interest on the whole if they hadn't been discouraged at the outset by the general mood of despondency that seemed to swamp the political spheres as well as by the oft-repeated assurance that the European Parliament was powerless and useless anyway. This turned out to be an unfair, and at least partly untrue, description, as events were to prove in later years.

Just prior to the elections, in March, the second important event of 1979 occurred: eight of the nine EC countries introduced the EMS, the European Monetary System, with a view to

(*Lomé: capital of the African State of Togo)

creating a modicum of stability amongst the various currencies by coordinating exchange-rate mechanisms. The United Kingdom was the odd man out. The EMS was based on the use of a common means of payment known as the ECU, the European Currency Unit (see page 48). As we know, the ECU was to become one of the major currencies for international transactions.

In 1981, the Nine became Ten, when Greece joined the EC, to be followed in January 1986 by Spain and Portugal.

In the thirteen years that had followed the entry of the UK, Ireland and Denmark, the building of the European Community had never stopped. However, bringing in more builders seemed to have the effect of slowing down the process rather than giving it the renewed impetus one had hoped for. There were constant squabbles and recriminations, chauvinism was rampant, every European discussion seemed to be organized solely to enable each national leader to go back home and explain how he – or she – had put one over the rest of the bunch. This attitude had very tangible and unfortunate results: Europe began losing ground behind the United States and Japan, it had great difficulty in climbing out of the economic crisis, unemployment remained obstinately high, economic growth was slower, and so were investments. Even though it plodded on, the European Community didn't seem to know where it was going. The objectives laid down by the Treaty of Rome seemed just so many empty shells. The people of Europe were disappointed and frustrated, although they remained very much alive to the importance of European unity. But it looked as if Europe had got itself into a cul-de-sac and was incapable of finding a way out. Euro-pessimism was rife.

This was the depressing picture Jacques Delors was faced with when he became President of the European Commission on 1 January 1985.

TONGUE-TIED YOUNG BRITONS

With the exception of ex East Germans and the Irish, young Britons aged between fifteen and twenty-four are worse than the rest of their European counterparts at being able to hold a conversation in any foreign language. A 1991 report on 'Young Europeans' published by the Commission in Brussels found that only 50% of a random sample of young Britons had any knowledge of a foreign language. The best result came from young Luxembourgers who spoke an average of 2.7 foreign languages each. They were followed in proficiency by the Danes (1.8), the Dutch (1.6) and the Belgians (1.1).

In the ranking of importance of languages young Europeans would like to learn, English dropped from first to fourth place between 1987 and 1990. Top ranking choice of languages in the survey was German.

9 Deadline 1993

Jacques Delors' nomination occurred at the very moment when the European leaders had started looking for ways to hoist the Community out of its seemingly chronic crisis which was threatening to become terminal.

In the spring of 1984, the Heads of State and Government gathered for their regular European summit at Fontainebleau, near Paris – they agreed that unless action was taken drastically and speedily, the Community might just as well fold up. They therefore decided that the keyword, the main objective from there on was to be: integration. The march towards an integrated Europe was to be resumed with a vengeance seeing as how the only alternative was total dis-integration of the whole Community system. By 'integration', European leaders meant that, once Spain and Portugal joined the EC as had been agreed, everybody's efforts should be aimed at strengthening all possible bonds between the twelve member States rather than bringing in still other members, which would very probably result, at that stage, in the Community becoming a vast and amorphous body with no real consistency, a sort of second-hand free trade association.

The question was obviously how to get this new phase of European construction off the ground. When Jacques Delors took over from the Belgian Gaston Thorn at the head of the Commission, he started off by exploring the various roads towards integration, if only to see how many were actually practicable. He realized he was, to all intents and purposes, at a crossroads: there were literally four roads leading off from where he stood.

First of all, he could try to obtain more power for the European institutions *vis-à-vis* the individual member States. That road had been tried in the past and had led nowhere, if not to squabbles, recriminations and chauvinistic attitudes. Eventually, the European institutions would have to have more power if the system was to continue working, but it would be easier if that occurred as the inevitable outcome of stronger European unity, instead of trying to make it the springboard for such unity.

A second possibility was to try immediately for a common currency. There again, the idea was attractive but it would imply dramatic political decisions that no government was then prepared to take, so it would certainly lead to years of useless haggling while nothing much happened elsewhere.

Thirdly, Jacques Delors could go all out for a common European defence. Everybody agreed that the principle of such a defence was appealing but nobody was prepared to jeopardize Europe's immediate security by quarrels on NATO or nuclear weapons, that would only emphasize its disunity in the eyes of the world. On top of which, the Commission is not empowered to take initiatives on defence.

So the best, in fact the only wise, solution that remained was to continue down the road the Europeans had been following since the Treaty of Rome which was meant to lead to a single market. Instead of changing roads, Jacques Delors thought it would be simpler and more effective to change pace, and speed up the journey. As every managing director, or indeed every news editor knows full well, the best way to get people moving is to set them a deadline.

In his maiden speech to the European Parliament in January 1985, the new President therefore outlined two significant objectives the Commission would be aiming for: in the short term, laying down the rules for a single market, thus making it irreversible; in the medium term achieving this market at the exact date of 31 December 1992.

These proposals met with universal approval. True to the Jean Monnet doctrine, they were simple and straightforward – at least in their general principles; they didn't, apparently, lead to national pride being hurt and they didn't seem to be treading on any political toes. As for the ordinary people of Europe, they discovered that there was still, in this day and age, something to strive for, all together, something that wasn't just pie in the sky but a definite plan that would, with a bit of luck and lots of goodwill, really put the old Continent back on the map. As for European businessmen, they were, on the whole, delighted. For years they had been convinced that all these trade and business barriers still in place all over Europe were a terrible hindrance and were largely responsible for our straggling behind the United States and Japan. Economists were delighted, because they had worked out how much this lack of unity was costing the EC in terms of money, but also in terms of jobs. The figures are significant enough to warrant a small diagram.

The suppression of trade barriers would allow the Community to save the following amount of money:

– Suppression of border controls and resulting red tape $\longrightarrow$	Money saved: 13/25 billion ECUs = £8.5/£16.5 billion
– Opening up of public procurement $\longrightarrow$	17.5 billion ECUs = £11.5 billion
– Reduction of industrial costs $\longrightarrow$	2% of Gross Domestic Product (GDP)

On the whole, it has been worked out that the total economic benefit for the European Community would work out as some 200 billion ECUs, i.e. around £120 billion, and bring about an increase in GDP of about 5%. This would open up the market to some two to five million potential jobs, and bring down consumer prices by about 6%.

Without even taking into account all the human or social issues, a real, honest-to-goodness single market would bring enough economic improvement to the Community as a whole to justify some effort in trying to achieve it.

The various European partners were by now so convinced of this that, in March 1985, the European Heads of State expressly instructed the Commission to put together before the next Council session a detailed programme and an agenda for setting up the Single Market. The Commission worked flat out and by

14 June had elaborated a complete draft of a document known as 'The White Paper on the Single Market'. This document was presented by Lord Cockfield (who was one of the British Commissioners) to the Heads of State and of Government when they met for the European Council session in Milan on 28 and 29 June.

The White Paper started off by stating the main objective: the blending of the twelve national markets into a single market of 320 million consumers by 31 December 1992. Once this objective was accepted, there was to be no turning back. The way of achieving this objective, said the White Paper, was to list, then eliminate, the physical, technical and tax barriers that represented an obstacle to the establishment of the Single Market. Having said that, the authors of the paper proceeded to spell out 282 specific legal measures that were necessary to eliminate those barriers.

Another important point was made: if the Single Market was to be a success, it had to remain flexible and capable of improvement and development, so that it would always be possible to adapt it as time went on and situations changed.

The White Paper underlined the differences between barriers – some were simply technical disparities that could be sorted out by equally technical measures; others would need profound changes covering vast economic areas. Finally, there would need to be accompanying measures in other fields – certain economic or trade decisions would automatically involve areas like the environment, consumer protection, citizens' rights, agriculture, jobs, etc. It was therefore important to provide the relevant legislation in these other areas when necessary, otherwise the ensuing confusion would lead to member States taking their own separate measures and making things even more complicated than before.

For instance, eliminating passport control at borders within the Community was obviously impossible unless the appropriate measures were taken to avoid criminals, terrorists or illegal immigrants cruising from one EC country to another without anybody being able to stop them; drug control was another problem that needed preliminary sorting out; also, sanitary control for animals being carted around Europe (what with rabies, mad cow disease, equine plague, to name but a few of the problems linked with animals, European vets wouldn't have known which way to turn . . .).

The White Paper also insisted on the importance of increasing free circulation of services in the same proportion as goods, because they are just as important to the general economy as industry or finance.

All the 282 measures proposed were to be examined and amended, adopted or rejected according to a precise calendar. Most of them were to be sorted out in the following three to four years, thus leaving ample time for each member State to make the necessary legal changes.

On the whole, the White Paper met with general approval; but problems immediately arose when it came to deciding on the institutional changes that would be needed to bring about the Single Market. Even though the project was entirely in the spirit of the Treaty of Rome, certain modifications and amendments had to be made to the original text.

The Milan European Council also had difficulty agreeing on ways and means of working towards a greater political cooperation, in fields such as security and foreign affairs, with a view to adding a few bricks to the European Union. Why foreign affairs, and what does that have to do with a single market? A lot, as it turns out, if one considers that a country's foreign affairs are in large part governed by its foreign trade, and vice versa. Eliminating trade and customs barriers between EC countries implies that barriers between the Community and the rest of the world must be standardized. On what basis? That of the more protectionist or of the more liberal EC countries? What policy as regards immigration? What about political asylum? And extradition agreements? etc., etc. One thing immediately leads to another, one thread pulled out means other threads coming loose, and it becomes very difficult to decide where to draw the line.

Finally, after lengthy discussions, a compromise was reached: each global decision would be based on the measures that were immediately necessary to the building of the Single Market, as well as the unavoidable side-measures and a basic, minimalistic amount of political cooperation. In other words, political decisions would be strictly limited to those absolutely indispensable to the completion of the Single Market, to be taken on a sort of day to day basis, instead of trying to cobble together the vast structure of a Political Union.

On the basis of this compromise, the next European Council, meeting on 2 and 3 December 1985 in Luxembourg, agreed on a draft for a treaty modifying certain points of the Treaty of Rome. After a last bout of tidying up by the Council of Ministers for Foreign Affairs on 17 December in Brussels, the Treaty was signed in Luxembourg on 17 February 1986 by the plenipotentiaries of nine member States (Mrs Lynda Chalker for the UK) and in The Hague on 28 February by those of the three remaining members – Denmark, Greece and Italy. The latter three had awaited the results of a referendum on the Single Act being held in Denmark. Danish voters approved the text by a 56.2% majority on 27 February.

Still the Treaty did not take effect immediately. The Irish Supreme Court had declared that it did not conform to the Irish Constitution. There again, a referendum was organized in Ireland which resulted, on 26 May 1987, in a 69% majority vote in favour of the Single Act. So, it was finally implemented on 1 July 1987.

THE SINGLE ACT

One of the fundamental points of the Single Act is that it gives the various Community institutions the means to achieve the Single Market without being uselessly hampered by certain procedures which had until then been responsible for the lack of impetus in the development of the EC.

Thus, the Treaty extends to a great variety of fields the possibility for the Council of Ministers to adopt a measure by a simple majority or qualified majority vote instead of a unanimous one. This resulted in a whole series of measures being adopted very quickly whereas, beforehand, some quite secondary problem – like, say, sugar in jam – could bring everything to a halt for months on end because one country was digging its heels in.

Unanimity is still required on a few specific subjects, including tax. Wisely, these subjects were left to last, so that they didn't hamper the initial move towards the Single Market and were discussed at a stage when it seemed very difficult, even psychologically, to jeopardize everything a few months from the final deadline.

The qualified majority system will also apply after 1992, when a general census throughout the member States will give a precise idea of all the dispositions that still have to be taken because they were not included in the 282 measures. At that point, the Council will have to adopt, by a qualified majority vote, the 'mutual recognition' rule, stipulating that dispositions existing in one member State on any given subject will be accepted by all the others as the equivalent of their own.

Another important point settled by the Single Act Treaty concerns the extent of the Commission's powers when it comes to executing the decisions taken by the Council. It was decided that the Council of Ministers could delegate its executive powers to the Commission – meaning that the Council takes a decision on an overall measure and leaves it up to the Commission to sort out the details.

The Single Act does not give the European Parliament the power it has consistently demanded to actually initiate and vote laws, but it does get to play a stronger role in the sense that the approval of Parliament is necessary for a new member to be accepted into the EC and for associations or agreements with outside countries to be concluded. There are also many decisions in which Parliament is more closely involved by means of the 'cooperation procedure', whereby it must be consulted by both Commission and Council before a final decision is made on a particular subject.

Once the Treaty has been signed – and it was already a great step forward for the Twelve to have agreed on the basic principles of the Single Market – it became a question of taking the practical measures necessary to get the whole system working. In February 1987, before the Single Act was signed, the Commission submitted a series of proposals known as the 'Delors package' that, as it were, set the stage for the implementation of the Act. This included a redefinition of the common agricultural and the European regional policies and a reform of the Community's financing mechanisms by adapting the contributions of the member States to their economic situation.

It took three consecutive European Councils for the Delors package to be finally adopted; after a first favourable reaction at the Brussels summit of June 1987, it was torn apart amidst violent discussions at the Copenhagen meeting in December. Things looked very bleak until a special European Council meeting in February 1988, in Brussels, patched everything up again.

As regards the common agricultural policy, it was decided to clamp down on spending, without, however, going so far as to dismantle the whole system; the Regional Fund, on the other hand, was allocated greater financial resources, as was the Community in general, though a stricter budgetary discipline was to be enforced. This modified package was accepted by everybody, and became known as 'the new Community contract'.

Better still, by the time the European Council met again in June at Hanover, a third of the 282 Single Market dispositions had already been implemented, thanks to the work of the Commission, the European Parliament and the Council of Ministers.

In fact, things had reached a 'point of no return', stated the European Council, who decided the time was ripe for starting work on an eventual monetary union. The Heads of State and government, who were in a decidedly good mood at the time, also committed themselves officially to developing the 'social and human dimension' of a united Europe.

At the next summit, held in Rhodes in December 1988, the Twelve agreed on a common 'philosophy' regarding the Community's commercial attitude towards the rest of the world. In answer to various accusations and preoccupations that had surfaced in other countries, the Council solemnly stated that there was to be no 'fortress Europe'; however, they warned, neither was the Community going to be open house for all and sundry.

THE SCHENGEN AGREEMENT

All this backslapping, nevertheless, could not hide the fact that there were still areas of grave dissent, notably on tax and on free circulation of private individuals between member countries. But, on this second point, progress was actually being made, through a parallel series of talks and agreements that involved only part of the twelve Community countries. It had all started off (as it had at the very beginning of the European Community) with France and Germany taking matters into their hands and getting to work on a bilateral agreement. At the Fontainebleau summit of June 1984, which had started the ball rolling towards the Single Market, one of the elements of European 'integration' considered as a major objective by the Heads of State was the idea of eliminating police and customs control at the borders between the Community countries. Four years later, at the Rhodes summit, a general consensus on the question was still miles away – yet what was to become the Schengen agreement was already on its way. In July 1984, barely a month after the Fontainebleau summit, France and Germany signed a first document, the Sarrebrück agreement, committing themselves to working towards the suppression of controls at their own common borders. By the following June, the two countries had been joined in this commitment by Belgium, Luxembourg and the Netherlands, and, on 14 June, in the little Luxembourg town of Schengen, they all signed a preliminary agreement specifying their intention of eliminating all obstacles hindering the free cross-border circulation of their citizens.

Several years of hard work were necessary for the preliminary agreement to become an official convention. Before eliminating border controls, it was necessary to take the appropriate measures for ensuring the security of the citizens of these five countries against terrorism, gangsterism, drug trafficking, etc. The five Schengen countries therefore agreed on a series of measures establishing, for instance, common extradition procedures and defining the principles of judicial cooperation. These 'judicial cooperation' procedures will be applied to facilitate police enquiries and the shadowing of suspects from one country to another. Exchanges between members of the various police forces are constantly being organized, so as to promote a better knowledge of one another's work methods. The same goes for customs officials, since the same customs rules have to be applied everywhere along the borders between the Schengen countries and the rest of the world. In certain cases concerning specific crimes (murder, rape, kidnapping, drug smuggling), police from one country will be entitled to pursue suspects into another, but not to arrest them, so a national police force will immediately have to swing into action.

It was decided to put together a computerized filing system listing all known dangerous criminals, all persons involved in drugs or arms traffic, all persons actively sought under the terms of a judicial enquiry, as well as people who have disappeared and absconding minors. This filing system will be open to the police and magistrates of the various Schengen countries to facilitate cooperation in the fight against crime.

Another difficult point was immigration control. Three types of measures were prepared:

– common rules and regulations would apply when deporting individuals residing illegally in any one of the countries involved;

– judicial measures against those responsible for bringing in illegal immigrants would be harmonized, though not necessarily standardized;

– the ways and means of escorting foreign nationals out of the country once their right of residence had been rejected would be subjected to precise legislation, making sure that the Geneva Convention of political asylum was respected.

As far as asylum itself was concerned, each country would retain its own laws and criteria, provided they were in agreement with the Geneva Convention; any request for asylum submitted to two or more Schengen countries would be examined by only one, who would have overall responsibility for the final decision.

Apart from this question of asylum, the Schengen agreement does not cover residence in another of the countries concerned, only travel.

The fall of the Berlin Wall in 1989 and the subsequent unification of Germany led to the Schengen agreement being put on the back burner for a while, to give the Germans time to sort themselves out. But discussions soon took up again and the final Schengen Convention was signed on 19 June 1990, with a view to being implemented in the summer of 1992. Italy, Spain and Portugal joined the group and added their signatures to the Convention: in November 1990 for Italy, in June 1991 for the other two.

All these separate discussions and agreements were never considered as a hindrance to the construction of a united Europe by the Community countries as a whole. They actually helped the Twelve come to certain agreements, such as deciding which country would be responsible for examining a request for asylum submitted in one of the EC States. This agreement was signed in June 1990 by eleven of the Twelve, and the following year by the twelfth, namely Denmark.

Another consequence of the upheavals in Eastern Europe was the decision taken by the Strasbourg European Council of December 1989 to set up a special financial organization, the European Bank for Reconstruction and Development (BERD), aimed at rationalizing and structuring the financial and economic aid the Community as a whole could give the Eastern European States. The Bank has its headquarters in London and is directed by a Frenchman (another one? absolutely), Jacques Attali, one of President François Mitterand's personal advisers.

The Strasbourg summit and the following one in Dublin in June 1990 also took some important steps in two vital directions: monetary union and political unity, by deciding to set up two 'intergovernmental conferences' whose job it would be to prepare the amendments to the Treaty of Rome that would be necessary to bring about this double union, just like the Single Act had amended a number of articles of the Treaty. Consequently, the 'Intergovernmental Conference on Economic and Monetary Union' and the 'Intergovernmental Conference on Political Union' started work officially in December 1990. Nobody, however, was paying a great deal of attention, as the whole world was then focused on the events in Kuwait and Iraq that were to lead to the Gulf War. In fact, when diplomats, politicians and journalists did turn their attention to Europe, it was to loudly bemoan the lack of political unity or influence of the Community. Whereas, until then, the word 'political', linked to the EC, had been like a red rag to a bull for most world leaders and media people (the British press and politicians being a good case in point), suddenly everybody was blaming the Community for not being a united political force – conveniently forgetting that there is no EC institution entitled to take political decisions or action; that can only be negotiated on a nation to nation basis.

Luckily, over the years, Community leaders and executives have grown quite used to the fickleness and injustice of public opinion towards them, and they did what they always do – they doggedly went on thrashing out the problems and striving towards the objectives that had been given them. The European Council, meeting in Luxembourg on 28 and 29 June 1991, took stock of progress achieved since the two conferences had started work in December of the preceding year.

June 1991 was also a good time for Community executives to examine what had been done and what remained to be done on the question of the Single Act, just before the last lap towards 1993.

Of the 282 measures outlined in the 1985 White Paper, 220 had been sorted out and adopted by the Twelve. This represented 75% of the total list. It did not imply, however, that the 220 measures had been implemented within the twelve member States. A great effort had nevertheless been made and, globally, some 72% of the 220 dispositions had been implemented (as opposed to 67% in December 1990), though proportions varied considerably according to each country. The slowest in transferring European measures into national legislation was Italy, who had hardly reached a total of 50%. On the whole, the results were very positive. There remained, nevertheless, some very serious problems to be solved, such as free circulation of individuals (since the Schengen Convention does not apply to all the member States), direct and indirect taxation (especially VAT), financial services, transport by air, road and sea, workers' rights and the creation of a new legal business entity, that of European Company.

Of course, if all these dossiers are not sorted out by 31 December 1992, one can assume that work will still go on and that, little by little, the problems will be solved. The difficulty, however, is that the Single Market cannot be operational as such unless every one of the 282 measures has been adopted – all it needs is for one barrier to remain and the Market will not be able to function as a single entity. Worse still, the Single Act will be seen as a failure and Europe will have lost the opportunity to figure as a world power.

10 The family album

WHO'S WHO

'We don't want to be bossed about by a load of Brussels bureaucrats', or, alternatively, 'a gang of Eurocrats', is a favourite battlecry with certain homegrown politicians as well as the more 'popular' press. Immediately, and certainly not fortuitously, our minds conjure up nightmarish visions of blank-faced, grey-suited figures lined up behind miles of identical desks, locked away in some vast anonymous bunker under the streets of Brussels, endlessly rubber-stamping piles of documents to the rhythmic crack of a whip wielded by a gimlet-eyed Jacques Delors. Shades of George Orwell . . .

That, of course, is when they're not all wallowing in lakes of champagne and mountains of caviar, lighting cigars with blazing fifty-pound notes, and generally living it up in the 'European gravy train' at the exclusive expense of the British ratepayer – the rest of the EC population having managed to avoid contributing a single penny thanks to the mysterious workings of the Common Agricultral Policy.

Slightly far-fetched, perhaps, but a very successful method, nevertheless, of giving the public preconceived ideas on a subject the majority know nothing, or very little, about. And yet, all those people responsible for the running of the Community have not, one assumes, sprung out of the earth like dragon's teeth or fallen from Mars like so many little green men: they are part and parcel of the population of Europe, including the UK. Like the majority of Europeans, including the British, they mostly try to do their jobs to the best of their ability in a context that is not always encouraging.

Getting to know the European Community means, thankfully, meeting the men and women, not the robots, who contribute to its progress. There are basically three large categories of people in the EC family album: civil servants, executives appointed by their respective governments, and elected representatives.

Civil servants

They represent the largest group, dubbed the 'Eurocrats'. All in all, there are some 25,000 Eurocrats working, on a permanent or a temporary basis, for the Community – around 15,000 for the European Commission (10,000 in Brussels, 2,400 in Luxembourg, 2,600 in other European locations), and the other 10,000 distributed between the European Parliament, the Council of Ministers, the Social and Economic Committee, the Court of Justice, the Court of Auditors and the European Investment Bank.

Considering that the European Community boasts some 340 million inhabitants, and considering the amount of work needed to keep the European ball rolling as smoothly as humanly possible, 25,000 civil servants do not add up to a vast administrative body. As a point of comparison, according to Richard Hay, head of personnel at the European Commission,★ the Lord Chancellor's Department in Britain or the Ministry of Culture in France employ around 10,000 people, and there are less civil servants in the European Commission than in the official services of the towns of Amsterdam or Madrid. So, on the whole, there are less people working for the EC than for, say, three major European town authorities put together.

This relatively small number of employees is mainly due to the fact that the European civil service began its existence in the 'fifties and is therefore very young compared to most national administrations, many of whom have been around in one form or another for generations, and even centuries. Consequently, it benefited from a more-up-date and sophisticated organization which enables it to use a smaller number of people more

(★ *The European Commission and the Community Administration*, EC Documents)

efficiently. It also needs to be very flexible: each entry of a new member State into the EC does not automatically mean adding large batches of civil servants from that country to the already existing numbers, but it does imply a minimum of reshuffling at certain levels of the administration. The structure has to be adaptable, so that the newcomers fit in as smoothly as possible and there is no question of responsibilities overlapping and of people treading on one another's toes.

The Community has total control over its administration, for the simple reason that it has its very own civil service. The alternative would have been for each national civil service to detach a stated amount of its own members to Brussels, Luxembourg or elsewhere; however, from the very beginning, this idea was rejected because it was feared that civil servants recruited by their own government would not have enough independence and could be pressurized into working for the sole benefit of their native country, as opposed to that of the EC.

Aside from independence, efficiency was another major criterion. European civil servants have to be very good at their job to be able to cope, over and above the usual workload, with the difficulties of multinational and multicultural relationships, different languages, mentalities and habits, and, for quite a few, the personal stress of leap-frogging from one point of the European map to another.

The best way to get efficient people is usually to pay them well so, when the European Community came into existence, it was decided to offer salaries capable of luring the right people away from the temptations of the private sector. This was true particularly at the start – now, Community salaries have been caught up with and overtaken in many fields of private industry and business and even national civil servants are slowly bridging the gap, especially in the higher-paid posts.

There are four main categories of civil servant.

– The top level is classified as Category A; a university degree is required from those who aspire to it. As with the other categories, it is divided into several grades (in this case eight), according to each individual's functions and responsibilities. The highest grade is A1, which corresponds to Director General. Within each grade are several echelons; employees move up an echelon every two years. Within the highest grade, A1, the highest echelon is A1–6. At this level, basic monthly salary amounts to some £6,850. The lowest salary for Category A is paid to echelon A8–1 and is around £1813 a month.

These were the salaries quoted in 1988 – but they haven't varied much since.

– Category B is divided into five grades, with eight echelons each (except grade B5, subdivided into only five echelons). To be integrated directly into Category B, you need an end of school diploma (A levels in Britain, Baccalauréat in France, Maturità in Italy, etc.). This category mainly includes middle-rank executives, like office manager or assistant. Basic salaries vary from £1,338 a month for a B5 to £3,292 a month for a B1–8.

– Category C mainly concerns secretaries, stenographers and typists; O level studies or their equivalent are required. There again, the category is divided into five grades and subdivided into echelons. The lowest basic salary, for a C5–1 employee, is £1,032 a month, the highest, for a C1–8, is £1,958.

– Finally, Category D is mainly made up of manual or service workers (cleaners, messengers, etc.), with four grades and four to eight echelons. Monthly salaries start at £933 for a D4–1 worker and reach a top level of £1,523 for a D1–8.

These main categories don't concern only administrative jobs. The EC procedures cover practically every spectrum of human activities, so it needs to employ a certain number of specialists in such fields as economics, law, human and animal health, nuclear security, etc.; also, most important, language specialists (interpreters, translators) without whom the system would grind to a halt in a matter of hours.

Contrary to what many people think – or say – European civil servants pay income tax, at a rate that goes from 15% for a basic monthly salary of £990 to 45% for a salary over and above £2,588 a month.

They contribute, of course, to a pension and a health scheme. They receive family allowance (around 5% of basic salary), child allowance (£102 a month per child) as well as a school allowance.

Employees who have to take up their job away from the country where they were recruited benefit from a special indemnity equal to 16% of the basic salary plus family and child allowance.

EC personnel are recruited yearly by means of entrance examinations. A certain amount of professional experience is required at all levels, as well as the capacity for living and working abroad. Exams, both written and oral, are open to candidates from all twelve EC countries. This means that they are held in the various languages of the Community, and in accordance with the various education systems. This inevitably leads to quite long delays before the results of the exams are made public. In the past, it could take up to two years, but now the delay usually lasts no more than a year, at the utmost.

In Categories B, C and D, nationality does not play a major role when it comes to recruiting personnel. Candidates are chosen strictly on the basis of their capability and experience in the best interests of the department involved. Things get more delicate when dealing with the upper echelons of Category A – it then becomes necessary to respect a certain balance between the nationals of all the different member States. This very understandable preoccupation can sometimes lead to a frustrating situation for certain high-ranking executives when they do not obtain the promotion they deserve because, at that particular stage, it was considered more diplomatic to favour a colleague of a different nationality.

Being recruited in a specific category and a specific grade within that category does not mean that an employee remains there for the rest of his professional life. Advancement is secured through the normal course of seniority or, very often, through internal exams.

As practically everywhere else, the Community employs more men than women, especially in the higher categories. In the lower and middle-ranking jobs, the balance of sexes is pretty well observed, but there are, as usual, very few women amongst top-level executives and decision-makers. It has therefore been decided, in particular within the European Commission services (the Commission being the largest single employer of the Community), to give precedence to women in Category A, when there are several candidates of equal competence for the same job. Women are also offered special training schemes so as to be able to progress from one grade, or one category, to another.

Nominees

The second large category to grace the family album is usually the one that gets the most flak from political and media circles in search of Euro-scapegoats. They are the top-ranking executives nominated by their respective governments or by the European Council of Ministers (which amounts to nearly the same thing, since the Ministers are members of national governments).

The ones best known to European newsreaders or television viewers are the seventeen members of the European Commission. France, Germany, Italy, Spain and the UK nominate two each, the other member States one. They are appointed for a period of four years, renewable. Once they have been nominated, they cannot be removed from their functions by anyone – with the exception of the European Parliament who can vote a motion of censure against the Commission, thus forcing all its members to resign. This has, as yet, never happened.

The seventeen men and women of the Commission are, in actual fact, the major force behind the European impetus, with power to initiate and execute policies, though not the power to adopt them.

The current President of the Commission, the Frenchman Jacques Delors, is probably one of the best-known figures in European politics since the time of his countrymen Monnet and Schuman. He is, temporarily, the figurehead of the Commission and is therefore often accused of being the walking, talking symbol of European bureaucracy, and even autocracy. Those who live and work alongside him do, in fact, admit that he is a hard taskmaster, for himself as much as for others and rather an aloof personality, not much given to hearty backslapping, even with his colleagues of the Commission. However, if the man himself commands rather an awestruck respect, his role as President does not put more power in his hands than in those of his sixteen colleagues, and the Commission's decisions are made collectively. As things stand right now, Jacques Delors' responsibilities cover: the Secretariat-General and Legal Service, Monetary Affairs, the Spokesman's Service, the Forecast Group, Joint Interpreting and Conference Service, the Security Office.

He is flanked by six Vice-Presidents:

– Frans Andriessen (the Netherlands), responsible for External Relations and Trade Policy, as well as Cooperation with other European countries;

– Martin Bangemann (Germany), in charge of Internal Markets and Industrial Affairs, as well as Relations with the European Parliament;

– Henning Christophersen (Denmark), responsible for Economic and Financial Affairs, Coordination of Structural Funds and the Statistics Bureau;

– Sir Leon Brittan (United Kingdom), in charge of Competition Policy and Financial Institutions;

– Manuel Marin Gonzalez (Spain), responsible for Cooperation and Development, as well as Fisheries Policy;

– Filippo Maria Pandolfi (Italy), in charge of Science, Research and Development, Telecommunications, Information industry and innovation, the Joint Research Centre.

The other ten Commissioners are:

– Carlo Ripa di Meana (Italy): Environment, Nuclear Safety and Civil Protection;

– Mrs Vasso Papandreou (Greece): Employment, Industrial Relations and Social Affairs, Human Resources, Education and Training, Relations with the Economic and Social Committee;

– Antonio Cardoso e Cunha (Portugal): Personnel, Administration and Translation, Energy and Euratom, Supply Agency, Small and Medium-sized Enterprises, Craft, Trade, Tourism;

– Karel Van Miert (Belgium): Transport, Credit and Investment, Consumer Protection;

– Abel Matutes (Spain): Mediterranean Policy, Relations with Latin America and Asia, North–South Relations;

– Peter M. Schmidhuber (Germany): Budget, Financial Control;

– Ray MacSharry (Ireland): Agriculture, Rural Development;

– Mme Christiane Scrivener (France): Taxation and Customs Union, Excise, Social Tax;

– Jean Dondelinger (Luxembourg): Audiovisual and Cultural Affairs, Information and Communication, Citizen's Europe, Official Publications Bureau;

– Bruce Millan (United Kingdom): Regional Policy.

The rest of the appointed executives work in three other European institutions:

– in the Court of Justice, thirteen judges and their assistants (six advocates-general) are appointed for six years by the various governments and by common consent;

– the Economic and Social Committee has 139 members. They are representative of the different economic and social fields, such as agriculture, transport, trade, crafts, trade unions, etc.; they are usually well-known and respected personalities, nominated for a period of four years by the Council of Ministers acting on the proposal of a specific government;

– the Court of Auditors is made up of twelve members, appointed for a period of six years by the Council, after the European Parliament has been consulted.

Elected representatives

Last but not least, the third category of European decision-makers is that of the 518 Euro-MPs. It has always been fashionable to consider that they have no power compared to that of the Eurocrats so, in a certain number of countries, many people don't even bother to go out and vote for them at election time. Since 1979, MEPs have been elected by direct universal suffrage, but not by the same voting system in every country. In the UK, the 81 MEPs are elected along the same principles as candidates for the House of Commons, i.e. the first-past-the-post system. In France, unlike national MPs, the 81 MEPs are elected by proportional representation, on party lists. This goes for Denmark, Germany, the Netherlands, Italy, Belgium and Luxembourg, with variations on the nature of the lists, divided sometimes into party, sometimes into regional, sometimes linguistic lists (this happens in Belgium, with Flemish and francophone lists). In Ireland, MEPs, like MPs, are elected by way of the 'single transferrable vote', a system used nowhere else in the world (except Tasmania!): voters choose their favourite candidate normally, but can also state who their second-favourite is; if candidate No. 1 has already got enough votes to ensure his election, the rest of his votes go to candidate No. 2, and so on. MEPs are elected for a period of five years.

As things now stand, the largest political group in the European Parliament is the Socialist group (180 members), followed by the European Popular Party or EPP (121 members), made up mostly of moderate right-wing representatives, with the exception of the British; there are 49 Liberals, 34 European Democrats (a group made up mainly of British Conservatives, with a sprinkling of Danes and Spaniards), 30 'Greens' and half-a-dozen smaller groups, ranging from the Communists to the extreme right-wing.

How do these Euro-MPs vote? It depends on the subject up for discussion. When 'practical' problems are being debated, like finance or agriculture, strange things have been known to happen, such as Italian Communists and British Conservatives casting the same vote, although more often national interests tend to come to the fore and the 81 French MEPs all gang up on their 81 British colleagues, or vice versa . . . When there are discussions on questions of principle, such as freedom of expression, the Rights of Man, etc., then political persuasions are generally observed and MEPs tend to obey party or group discipline.

Euro-MPs benefit from a double parliamentary immunity during the course of the European Parliament sessions: in their own country, they have the same immunity as their colleagues of the national Parliament; on the territory of any other member State, they are also immune from arrest, detention or any form of legal proceedings. This protection is extended to their trips to and from the European Parliamentary Assembly.

As far as their salaries are concerned, it was decided that it would be up to every national Parliament to fix a sum for the country's MEPs. This followed months of vociferous debates and press campaigns, spurred on by rumours that MEPs' salaries would be based on those of the best-paid national MPs, to whit the Germans. This controversy did a lot towards convincing the likes of us that European MPs were grossly overpaid and underworked. Actually, they are not paid any better or any worse than their national counterparts, since they get exactly the same salary. If an MEP is also a member of his national Parliament, he still only gets one salary – except in the Netherlands, where he is allowed both. The outcome, of course, is that some MEPs (the British in particular) are worse off than others, which is rather unfair and, what is more, contrary to the Treaty of Rome that forbids any form of discrimination, financial or otherwise, due to nationality. To try and compensate for this, the European Parliament has granted a few financial facilities to its MPs:

– each one is allocated an asssistant and a secretary, whose salaries are taken from the Community budget;

– a yearly non-taxable allowance of 4,800 ECUs (£3,600) covers various expenses, in particular all the comings and goings between the various European institutions and organizations;

– trips to and from the Parliament are also reimbursed and MEPs are issued a daily hotel and food allowance (around £50) when they are taking part in the Parliamentary sessions.

Anybody whose chief aim in life is to become a millionaire

might do well to think twice before standing for the European Parliament – at least long enough to become a millionaire first.

WHAT'S WHAT

Like any solid piece of furniture, the European Community stands on four legs, each bearing its equal share of the total load.

The Council of Ministers

Decisions on the whole range of European policy are made by the Council of Ministers. According to the subject being discussed, the Ministers vary. Agricultural questions, for instance, are examined and decided on by the Agriculture Ministers – or Secretaries – of the twelve member States. Every six months, the Council is presided over by a different member State – so, every Council meeting over that period is chaired by a Minister of that particular State in charge of the subject under discussion.

The Council's work is based on the proposals prepared by the European Commission, in the presence of the Commission member responsible for those particular proposals (Mrs Papandreou if it's Social Affairs, Mr MacSharry if it's Agriculture, Mr Pandolfi if it's Science, etc.). The final decision is put to a vote. Depending on the subject, it may be a unanimous vote, or a qualified majority vote.

A unanimous vote is necessary for adopting measures on three subjects: taxation, the free circulation of individuals and the rights of workers. For the rest, however, majority votes are sufficient; the qualified majority is most frequently required. Each country has a set amount of votes: France, Germany, Italy and the UK have 10 votes each; Belgium, Greece, the Netherlands and Portugal have 5, Spain has 8, Denmark and Ireland 6, Luxembourg 2. The total number of votes therefore amounts to 76. A proposal is adopted when it has obtained at least 54 favourable votes. A qualified majority means that the 54 favourable votes must be divided between at least 8 countries – this is to avoid a number of larger States pushing a motion through against the wishes of the smaller ones.

The Council of Ministers is assisted by a permanent body, COREPER (Committee of Permanent Representatives), made up of the ambassadors of the twelve member States and their aides. COREPER acts as liaison for the Council and the Commission in between meetings and prepares the work for the various Ministers.

The European Commission

The largest institution is the European Commission, with its 15,000 employees. Headed by the seventeen European Commissioners, it has a double mission: at the source, it must prepare and present all the proposals due to be examined and voted on by the Council of Ministers; once the decision has been made, it is up to the Commission to make sure that it is carried out inside the member countries.

The Commission is also responsible for the proper implementation of European treaties and any other judicial initiatives taken by the Community. If these treaties or initiatives are not observed as they should be, it can apply to the European Court of Justice. It has never hesitated to do so, whether against organizations, companies or governments. A typical and frequent case denounced by the Commission is that of a government giving special financial aid to a company and going against the rules of normal competition. The Commission, in the guise of Sir Leon Brittan (responsible for Competition Policy), never fails to pounce.

The main objective is – and must be – to defend on all counts the interests of the Community, in particular against national pressures that are often very strong. 'Abandon any national impulse, you who enter these doors' could be written in letters of fire over the portals of the Commission's conference room, where they gather once a week. It takes a strong personality and a great deal of integrity to withstand the pressures, the press campaigns, the lobbying, sometimes the insults the Commissioners are constantly being subjected to. Some of them have found themselves being snubbed by their own countrymen when returning home at the conclusion of their mandate for not having sufficiently 'defended the interests of their country', i.e. not having toed the official line decreed by their national institutions and politicians. Certain governments sometimes choose to misconstrue the role of the Commissioners, try to use them as advocates of their own national policies; when they realize they cannot bend them to their will, they brand them as autocrats, bullies, traitors, and other compliments to that effect. This can only mean that the Commissioners are doing their job very well!

In any case, they certainly do not have the time to sit about downing champagne, if the workload is anything to go by. In a normal year, the Commission can submit between six and seven hundred proposals to the Council of Ministers. These proposals cover all the numerous activities the European Community is involved with. On top of that, the Commission is responsible for managing common policies – such as the Common Agricultural Policy, Regional Development and Employment. It is also responsible for drawing up the Community budget, before submitting it to the Council and to Parliament. It can be given a mandate from the Council to negotiate trade agreements with non-member countries, such as the United States and Japan, and organize aid to developing countries belonging, or not, to the Lomé Convention. This has meant creating a special department just to manage customs and import questions.

The Commission itself is represented by some ninety delegations or bureaux throughout the world – in countries concerned one way or another with Community matters – as well as in international organizations.

A very important part of the Commission's activities is research. Initially, this was concentrated on coal and steel and on the non-military use of nuclear energy. This latter field of responsibility has been largely extended: it covers research on security, environment, satellite detection, systems engineering, advanced materials, carried out by the Common Research Centre in four separate establishments (at Ispra in Italy; Karlsruhe in Germany; Petten in the Netherlands; and Geel in Belgium). The European Community is also a partner in the **JET** programme, on the study of controlled nuclear fusion. The JET, or Joint European Torus, is a vast experimental system operating at Culham in the United Kingdom.

Research activities have given rise to many and varied European programmes in universities, institutes and firms. Thanks to programmes like **ESPRIT**, **BRITE** or **RACE**, a great deal of progress has been achieved in new technological fields, such as telecommunications and data processing.

The Commission – or, to be precise, its administration – is also responsible for linguistic affairs. This is a vital cog in the works. By common consent, no particular language has been adopted as the 'Community' language, because it is considered essential to the very spirit of the EC that each country retains its linguistic identity. There are, in fact, nine official languages since certain countries have a common one – Danish, Dutch, English, French, German, Greek, Italian, Portuguese and Spanish. This implies that every single document, every single agreement, proposal, information, speech, exchange, must be translated in such a way that it looks as if it had been originally written or spoken in each of the nine languages. The aim, says Richard Hay, is for every man and woman to feel an immediate familiarity with an EC document – they must be able to understand it is as easily as if it had been written in their native tongue.

It has been worked out that, in 1988, some 900,000 pages of EC documents were translated.

And translating written text is only one aspect of the linguistic juggling inherent to Community exchanges. Simultaneous interpretation at several hundred weekly meetings, conferences or discussions is carried out in a variety of languages, not necessarily just the nine European ones. This explains why the Commission employs some 460 interpreters and 1,200 translators, as well as around 650 assistants, e.g. typists to type the documents in all the different languages. All in all, there are some 2,700 people involved, in one capacity or another, in the business of dealing with languages.

The administrative services of the Commission are located in Brussels and Luxembourg. The seventeen Commissioners meet and work mainly in the Community's Belgian GHQ, although their various responsibilities often lead them to travel all over the world.

The European Parliament

Another European focal point is Strasbourg, where Community institution number three, the European Parliament, assembles. There again, language barriers can make life difficult, with members letting fly in nine different tongues – and a whole variety of accents – thus requiring the services of some 600 interpreters and translators from one end of the year to the next.

Since MEPs have been elected by direct suffrage since 1979, practically every adult citizen of the Community has at the very least heard of the existence of the European Parliament, though not many of them take the slightest interest in its role, its duties or the way it functions.

The Parliament has in fact existed since 1958, but the public didn't pay much attention to it, because, for twenty-one years,

Euro-MPs were chosen within their own national Parliaments. The ways and means of designating them varied – some countries, like Italy, would send to Strasbourg an identical number of MPs and Senators; some, like France, would send more MPs and less Senators; others, like Britain, would decide on the spur of the moment. When Britain first joined the Community, its only Euro-MPs were Tories, because Labour did not approve of the Heath negotiations and only became involved in 1975, after the referendum. As for the Tories, they tended to designate their Euro-MPs preferably in the House of Lords, so as to keep as many MPs as possible in the House of Commons, where the Conservative majority was not, at the time, large enough to allow many absentees at crucial voting sessions.

Today, it is no longer necessary to be a Member of Parliament to become an MEP. A lot of Parliamentarians still fulfil both functions, but an increasing number find it more and more difficult to play both cards, as the European Parliament's importance, influence and workload are very much on the increase.

However, it still lacks the major power inherent to national Parliaments, which is to lay down the laws of Europe. It is, however, consulted by the Commission on most of the proposals that will be put to the Council of Ministers, and its opinion on these questions is always taken into consideration.

The Parliament, as already stated, has the power to dismiss the Commission by means of a no-confidence vote that must be adopted by a two-thirds majority.

Since 1975, the Parliament has also been allotted bigger budgetary powers, such as increasing certain expenses suggested by the Commission. It cannot, however, initiate new means of financial returns. In other words, it can't invent and enforce new European taxes.

The Single Act, in 1987, gave yet more power to the Parliament by instituting a cooperation procedure in conjunction with the Council of Ministers, in certain areas where decisions are taken by a qualified majority. It now has a bigger say in such matters as technological research and development, social policies and trade within the Community.

Although the Parliament itself gathers in Strasbourg, its regular contacts with the Commission are made in Brussels, by means of a number of specialist committees, who interview the appropriate Commission member on his or her specialized subject and then report back to Strasbourg. The secretariat of the Parliament, on the other hand, is settled in Luxembourg. As during sessions the European Parliament is in assembly one week out of four, this compels MEPs to shuttle back and forth between Strasbourg and Luxembourg, when they're not rushing off to their constituencies back home. On the whole, becoming a European Member of Parliament is definitely not a career to recommend to anyone suffering from travel sickness . . .

This rather hectic situation has led to innumerable protests from MEPs, fed up with the agitation and loss of time due to all this shunting about; however, every time some possible discussion hovers in sight, Brussels, Strasbourg or Luxembourg start putting up such a vigorous resistance to any change benefiting one city to the detriment of the other two that everybody gives up after a lot of recrimination, snarling, and unpleasant remarks bandied about by Parliamentarians and immediately taken up by journalists across Europe. British MEPs are currently making a concerted effort to get Parliament transferred to Brussels because they consider it more convenient for themselves as it is nearer the UK. The French see this as another hostile manoeuvre against France. As for the Belgians, they seem quite happy at the idea of submitting Brussels to even heavier traffic jams than it already has to bear.

The affairs of Parliament are run by a President and fourteen Vice-Presidents gathered in a Bureau. They are all elected by their peers for a period of two and a half years.

It also has a very large and active Information Bureau whose object it is to encourage European citizens to learn all about their Parliament. Some 15,000 visitors are thus invited yearly, from all the Community countries, to Strasbourg. The Parliament also has Information Offices in all the EC capitals.

Its civil servants are recruited in the same way as for the European Commission, by means of a special exam specific to the Parliament, and through the administrative services of their own countries, always with the idea in mind of total independence from national pressures.

The Court of Justice

Independence is, of course, the keyword for the fourth major European institution: the Court of Justice. Also created by the Treaty of Rome, it sits in Luxembourg, where it is also lucky enough to have all its administrative services. Out of the thirteen Judges of the Court of Justice, twelve are nationals of each member State; the thirteenth is usually from one of the larger member countries. They elect a President of the Court amongst themselves. As stated earlier, they are flanked by six advocates-general, appointed by common decision of all member States. Judges and advocates-general are appointed for six years, but not for the same six years. Every three years, six Judges and three advocates-general are changed, so that the period of activity of one half is always overlapping by three years the period of activity of the other half. During these six years, they cannot be dismissed by anybody and have the same immunity from legal proceedings as that of Members of Parliament.

The European Court of Justice can be appealed to by a variety of groups or people – these include the European Commission, the Council of Ministers, governments from any of the EC countries, courts from any EC country and any group or individual belonging to one of the EC countries.

The role of the European Court of Justice is mainly to decide whether a given situation, ruling or initiative, is contrary to Community legislation and provisions.

When and how can an individual refer to the Court of Justice? Not directly. An individual involved in a court case in any EC country including his own can, at any moment, ask the magistrates or judges in charge of the case to put a 'preliminary question' to the European Court, asking it to decide whether a particular point in his case is or is not contrary to European legislation, or whether he is not suffering personal prejudice through some Community ruling. An individual can also appeal to the Court of Justice to obtain compensation for damages caused by an institution or an employee of the European Community 'during the course of their duties'.

The Court is the Community's supreme judicial authority, so there can be no appeal against its decisions; and these decisions overrule national laws and national courts.

European citizens and their lawyers, as well as European magistrates or judges, have not yet got into the habit of appealing to the European Court of Justice, but they are beginning to learn. In 1975, there were 135 cases referred to the Court; in 1987, there were 395. As the workload of the Court has increased, so has the delay in the judgement of each case. This can cause problems, because, if a preliminary question to the European Court is introduced during a national court case, that case is suspended until Luxembourg has made its judgement known. To make things quicker and easier, the Single Act has provided for a Court of First Instance, entitled to deal with certain specific problems: action brought for damages, action for unfair competition and cases referred by the Commission.

Many Europeans confuse the Court of Justice in Luxembourg with the European Court for the Rights of Man, which sits in Strasbourg. The Strasbourg Court is responsible for making sure that the twenty-one member countries of the European Council do not infringe the 1950 Convention for the Respect of the Rights of Man and of Civil Liberties; anyone living in one of the twenty-one States – except, as already stated, Cyprus, Malta and Turkey – can appeal to the Strasbourg Court, not directly but through the European Rights of Man Commission, if they consider that their basic rights have not been respected. It was the Strasbourg Court which ruled against caning in British schools.

Other institutions

Apart from the four major ones, there are a few other important institutions, even though not all of them are as well known.

   – *The European Council* was created by the Treaty of Rome, but it came into being in 1960 and proved to be so useful that it was institutionalized by the Single Act. It is, in actual fact, a twice-yearly gathering of the Heads of State or Government, to work out the major guidelines for Europe. It is often still called the 'Summit', preceded by the name of the town where it gathers. The Council meets each time in a different location, and is presided over by the leader of the country who, at that moment, happens to be filling in the six-months European presidency. It was the Council who came up with such vital initiatives as the Single Act, the European Monetary System or the wish for a European Political Unity.

   – *The Court of Auditors*, established in July 1977 in Luxembourg, examines the accounts of the Community, as well as the general budget. It verifies that returns and expenses are all correct and consistent with European legislation, and that Community funds are properly managed. It presents a yearly record of its activities to the other Community institutions. Its twelve members are appointed for six years by the Council of Ministers.

– *The Economic and Social Committee* is made up of 189 representatives of professional organizations and trade unions, and is based in Brussels. It is consulted by the Commission on proposals before they are submitted to the Council of Ministers and can suggest any change it considers useful or necessary. It can also, since 1972, make suggestions on its own initiative.

A special committee, the CECA Consultative Committee, is made up of representatives of the coal and steel industries, and is there to advise specifically on matters relating to these two activities.

– *The European Investment Bank*, set up by the Treaty of Rome, is the Community's financial institution for funding long-term projects. It helps finance these projects through loans and guarantees. It is also involved in the financing of the Community development policy and the distribution of funds, within or without the EC.

Another banking institution, the European Bank for Research and Development, based in London, specializes in financial help to the Eastern European States.

Finally, there are three smaller organizations, attached to the European Commission, which it can be useful to know about.

– *The Office for Official Publications*, responsible for publishing and distributing all the Community's official documents;

– *CEDEFOP*, the European Centre for Adult Education and Vocational Training, based in Berlin;

– *the European Foundation for Better Living and Working Conditions*, whose aims are pretty well explained by its rather lengthy title.

11 Figuring the cost

THE EC BUDGET

£99.50. That, give or take a few pence, represents the average amount contributed each year by every individual EC citizen towards the budget of the European Community. It may not seem exactly dirt cheap but, compared to what we fork out through direct and indirect tax, and social contributions, it works out at no less than thirty times cheaper.

Nonetheless, £99.50 is still £99.50, and we are entitled to know what the Community does with the money. For the benefit of those who still harbour visions of gravy trains and champagne lakes, here are a few simple figures that may be of interest:

In 1989, the total budget of the European Community amounted to 45 billion ECUs (we'll see later exactly how the EC gets this money), i.e. some £54.7 billion. This represents 3.5% of the total budget of all the member States and about 1% of their total GNP (Gross National Product, i.e. the global amount of revenue produced every year by the inhabitants of a country). Just as a point of comparison, if the national budgets of the twelve member States were clubbed together, it would come to some 2,500 billion ECUs a year.

Out of this 45 billion ECUs budget, less than 5% is attributed to functional expenses; so less than 2.2 billion ECUs are actually expended on the workings of the Community itself (such as the salaries of its 25,000 civil servants, travel expenses, printing and publishing of thousands of documents, etc.). The remaining 95% are redistributed, one way or the other, to all the member States.

The EC budget has grown over the years. In 1973, it came in at 0.5% of the European GNP instead of today's 1%, so it has doubled during those sixteen years, and even more than doubled if you take into account the fact that the Community itself has gone from six to twelve member States. This is mainly because common policies have grown in size and number – what used to be national policies (like agriculture) have been taken over by the EC authorities. So, quite logically, the money for financing these policies has also been taken over.

The immediate conclusion that can be drawn from this first set of figures is that the Community should not be seen as something 'extra', but as 'instead of'. In other words, the money spent by the Community authorities would have been spent on those same policies by the member States anyway, with the difference that it would have been done in a much more haphazard way, as each country would have had its own set of priorities.

Who is responsible for establishing the Community budget? Three of the main EC institutions are directly involved, to wit the Commission, the Parliament and the Council of Ministers; and the whole procedure takes about six months. It's a somewhat lengthy and complicated system, because it has to be overseen by all three institutions. The advantage, however, is that their involvement, in particular that of the European Parliament, is a guarantee of democratic control, since the Parliament is the EC citizen's best means of information and control.

Practically, this is how the system works. First of all, the European Commission works out a preliminary budget proposal based on the needs of the Community and its institutions, foreseeable receipts and (since 1986) multi-annual financial perspectives already approved by the Council and the Parliament. This document is submitted to the Council who adopts or amends it by a qualified majority vote (see page 162), thus turning it into an official project.

This project is then discussed by Parliament, who can *suggest* certain modifications, in the case of 'compulsory expenses' (those that cannot be avoided), or *adopt* amendments for those expenses that are not compulsory.

There is then a second budget examination by the Council, who must vote on the modifications proposed by Parliament that could lead to an increase in compulsory expenses. There again, a qualified majority is needed for them to be adopted, as well as for any amendments on non-compulsory expenses. If these amendments are rejected, Parliament can introduce them once again, and vote on them. It must make sure, however, that these amendments do not increase expenses to the extent that they go above the ceiling set by the multi-annual financial perspectives agreed on by the three institutions. Provided this ceiling has been respected, Parliament has the final say in the matter, since, after a second vote, the President declares the budget formally adopted. Of course, there is always the possibility that Parliament rejects the project – at which point everybody goes back to the drawing board, or, in this case, to their calculators.

This power to adopt or reject the budget – what is more, without having to refer to national Assemblies – is a very important aspect of the role of the European Parliament: if holding the purse-strings (in conjunction with the Council of Ministers) is not one of the most efficient ways of wielding power, then what is?

And what could be a better guarantee of democracy than to put that power into the hands of those who represent the citizens of Europe – or at least those who bother to vote? It might be a point to keep in mind when the next European Parliamentary elections come round – if people do not vote, aren't they less entitled to complain about the way their money is being spent?

There is one other institution whose job it is to control the legality and the validity of the Community's expenses and returns, as well as the administration of the budget, and that is the European Court of Auditors (see page 169).

The Commission has also created a special 'fraud squad' and has submitted to the Council a series of measures to prevent and punish frauds and irregularities that are sometimes committed by certain groups or people with a view to benefiting from Community subsidies. And there are quite a few of them, judging by the figures published by the Commission: it worked out, for instance, that in 1990, 1,190 cases of fraudulent activities cost the Community some 227 million ECUs (nearly £150 million). In general, the idea is either to avoid paying the taxes that go into the making of the Community budget or unduly benefiting from agricultural subsidies. In the first instance, it means issuing false documents stating that goods actually coming from outside the EC are being imported from one Community country to another; this avoids payment of entrance tax (see page 180). In the second instance, the usual trick is to issue, once again, false papers to the effect that a particular load of foodstuffs is being exported to a non-EC country where it is usually sold at a lower price, which means that the exporter will get compensation under the rules of the Common Agricultural Policy. In truth, those foodstuffs are sent to an altogether different country where they are sold at equal or higher prices than in the EC. So the exporter not only makes a profit, but gets a compensation he is not entitled to.

Other frauds are even nastier, because they are committed at the expense of human poverty or suffering. Like the case where the European Social Fund gave substantial subsidies for improving the appalling living and health conditions prevailing in a psychiatric institution in one of the EC countries. A year later, not an ECU had been spent . . . on that hospital.

All this seems pretty ghastly, and so it is; nevertheless, the fact that the frauds can be detected and the culprits publicly pinpointed is a very powerful weapon in the fight against malpractice and embezzlement. And, if and when the Commission is given the means to punish this misuse of public money quickly and efficiently, it will be even better.

How does the Community get its money? Most importantly, the Community finances its budget through its own resources, and does not have to count on the various national treasuries. This, as already stated, is a major guarantee of independence.

Within the EC the European Coal and Steel Community, the first of the European institutions, created in 1951, has its own operational budget (329 million ECUs in 1989). From the very first, this budget was financed by a European tax levied on the total production assets of all coal and steel enterprises. In 1989, this tax amounted to 0.31% of those assets.

At the beginning, following the Treaty of Rome, the European Economic Community and Euratom were financed by individual contributions from the member States, based on the respective GNPs. However, it had been stated from the start that the Community would have its own resources eventually, so, in 1970 it was decided to give it its own separate budget with its own distinctive returns, even though these returns are obtained through the administrative channels of each individual State.

There are four sources of Community income:

– The most important one is VAT. Each member State has to pass on to the EC 1.6% of its own VAT returns; there is however a ceiling for countries (like Greece, Portugal or the UK) where private consumption represents a very important part of national income. The portion of VAT transferred to the Community is not automatically calculated on the total VAT returns, but on a maximum of 55%; in other words, from a country where it represents less than 55% of national income, the Community gets 1.6% of total VAT returns; in a country where VAT represents 60, 70% or more of national income, the Community will get 1.6% of 55%.

VAT represents 61.6% of the Community's total receipts.

– The second most important source of income is represented by customs duties on imports into the Community from outside countries. It is important to stress that the Community is not at all concerned with excise duties between member States. This is perfectly logical since the whole idea is to abolish duties between member States, so it would be absurd for the Community to live off a tax it is supposed to eliminate.

On the other hand, you can imagine the complications if duties on outside goods had to be divided between the EC countries importing that product to the exclusion of the others. Complications, and also a good excuse for all sorts of fraud to be committed. It seemed much simpler to give the Community as a whole the benefit of these taxes. So, if you come back to London from Singapore or Tokyo with a complete stereo set, you will have the moral satisfaction of knowing that any duties you are paying will be for the ultimate benefit of 340 million Europeans – which is not the case if you have to pay duty on five bottles of perfume bought in Paris. It is therefore with a totally clear Euro-conscience that a man can limit his wife's consumption of her favourite French perfume to the 60 cc/ml allowed for the moment at Franco-British borders.

All in all, customs duties account for 23.4% of the Community's receipts.

– Levies on agricultural products imported, like the others, from outside the EC represent a further 3%. These taxes are aimed at aligning prices from outside countries with those practised within the EC. An additional tax is levied on sugar and certain types of glucose, wherever they come from, so as to limit surpluses. That brings in less than 2.8% of Community income.

– Finally, in 1988, the European Council introduced a new source of income based on the twelve countries' gross national product to help meet new expenses caused by the preparation of the Single Market. This represents something like 0.09% of the sum total of the twelve GNPs, although the proportion can vary each year. Each country contributes on the basis of its own GNP – that total is not, therefore, evenly divided by twelve. Each State pays according to its own national resource and, consequently, to what it can afford. The United Kingdom has special treatment here. Since Mrs Thatcher heatedly demanded her money back, in 1986, the Twelve agreed that Britain would pay less because it benefits less from agricultural subsidies than the rest of the Community. Without going into abstruse mathematical details, suffice to say that Britain pays out slightly less in VAT contributions.

This new source of income amounted, in 1989, to 9.2% of total budget receipts.

Here is a list of the receipts that the Community took in 1989:

	MILLIONS OF ECUs	%
Customs duties	9,954	22.2
Agricultural levies	2,462	5.4
VAT	26,219	58.5
GNP resources	3,907	8.7
Miscellaneous	274	0.6
Balance from previous year	2,025	4.5
TOTAL	44,841	

Where does the money go? The following diagram can give an idea of how Community spending has evolved from 1973 to 1989:

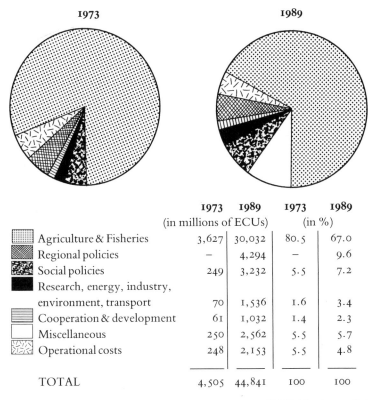

	1973	1989	1973	1989
	(in millions of ECUs)		(in %)	
Agriculture & Fisheries	3,627	30,032	80.5	67.0
Regional policies	–	4,294	–	9.6
Social policies	249	3,232	5.5	7.2
Research, energy, industry, environment, transport	70	1,536	1.6	3.4
Cooperation & development	61	1,032	1.4	2.3
Miscellaneous	250	2,562	5.5	5.7
Operational costs	248	2,153	5.5	4.8
TOTAL	4,505	44,841	100	100

(*EC Publications 11/89*)

As you can see, in those sixteen years the Community's total expenditure has been multiplied by ten. During that same time, consumer prices in the Community increased fourfold. However, since 1973, the number of EC States went from six to twelve and, since 1985, the drive towards the Single Market could not have succeeded without appropriate financing.

Practically, expenses are divided thus:

● 67% of the budget goes to agriculture and fisheries (57% being spent on guaranteeing farm prices). The size of their share in the Community budget is due to the fact that agriculture and fisheries are the two areas that obtain hardly any national financing now, and practically everything from the EC.

● Regional and social expenditure are the second most important expenditure. The money goes to three major funds (although, as you will have noticed throughout the book, there are many other smaller ones): the Regional Fund, the Social Fund, the European Agricultural Guidance and Guarantee Fund. These three funds took up slightly over 22% of expenses in the 1989 budget. By 1993, they should be getting even more money, as they are considered a very efficient means of coordinating Community action in view of the Single Market.

• Areas such as research, environment, industry, etc. are getting more financing than they used to, but it is still far from ideal: 3.4% of total expenditure is certainly better than nothing, but the Community authorities are well aware that the Single Market would be seriously handicapped if it were not building up a solid and coherent technological base, at the same time as a unified economy. Europe is still lagging behind in the technological race and this, as we all know, affects its economic development.

• Development aid (2.3% of expenditure) increased by 18% between 1988 and 1989. Most of this goes towards food aid to Mediterranean countries, Asia and Latin America. This money, however, is not invested in the activities of the Lomé Convention, i.e. financial and technical aid to the sixty-six countries from Africa, the Caribbean and the Pacific that signed the Convention. This particular aid is financed separately by the European Development Fund, which gets its money directly through national contributions.

• As for miscellaneous expenses, they consist mainly in reimbursements to various member States, for a variety of reasons (like when Britain 'wants her money back').

• And, as already stated, some 5% of the budget goes to operational expenses, i.e. the actual day to day running of the Community.

THE MAJOR EXPENSES OF THE COMMUNITY

1. Agriculture and fisheries

Agriculture

The Common Agricultural Policy (CAP) has, for years, been

the bugbear of the press, an election theme for politicians and a permanent occasion for imaginative and sometimes violent demonstrations by farmers all over Europe. And yet, strange as it may seem, agriculture has been one of the Community's great success stories. The problem now is that, if Europe's agricultural policies cannot be adapted to the present situation, then we are definitely heading towards failure. What we Europeans hear today is that more and more money is being poured into an area where fewer and fewer people are employed, and those who are cannot reap the benefits of this money – on the contrary, their situation is getting worse. As a matter of fact, the *relative* amount of expenditure has gone down (as is obvious from the diagram on page 177), although the amount in *absolute* figures went up ten times in sixteen years. In 1973, agriculture and fisheries cost the Community 3,637 million ECUs, but represented more than 80% of total expenditure; in 1989, they cost more than 30 million ECUs, but had gone down to 67% of total expenditure.

At the same time, the number of farmers was regularly decreasing. In 1960, the six original member States had over 17 million people living off the land; by 1987, always in the same six countries, they were down to 5.2 million. Now, in the Community of twelve, there are on the whole some 10 millon people involved in agriculture. Yet, even as the number of farmers diminished, productivity increased, to the extent that European agricultural policy is today, in a sense, a victim of its own success.

When the Common Market became an objective, in the early fifties, Western Europe was just managing to struggle out of the terrible food penury and restrictions due to the war. What one must remember is that, towards the end of the fifties, the 17 million farmers of the original Community worked 160 million acres of land to feed a population of 150 million people, while at the same time, in the USA, some 980 million acres were cultivated to feed 200 millon people and in the Soviet Union, 1.5 billion acres went to feed 250 million people. An American farmer owned on average 250 acres, enabling him to feed 50 people, while his European counterpart, with 20 times less arable land, could only feed 10 people. Europe, at the time, couldn't produce enough to feed itself, never mind exporting!

One of the main ideas of the Community's Founding Fathers was that never again should Europe go hungry, which is why so much energy and creativity went into developing agriculture. And it worked. Productivity has never stopped growing; today, concentration and specialization of agricultural activities, intensive production methods, improved varieties and rationalized distribution have made agriculture capable of supplying over and above the needs of Europeans and of exporting vast amounts of products outside the Community. As a matter of fact, in 1990, surplus stocks for certain products had reached alarming proportions (20 million tons of cereals, 750,000 tons of beef, 900,000 tons of milk products). In any normal market situation, a number of farmers would by now be totally ruined, because all this over-production would make prices plummet. However, it doesn't happen quite that way, because the Community strives to keep prices at a certain level, to avoid enormous fluctuations due to over-production, but also to avoid penury due to floods, frost or any other act of God.

At the same time, there is what is known as 'Community preference', which consists of helping the EC food production to sell abroad and at home – taxes on incoming foodstuffs bring their prices up to Community level (so that, say, an orange from Israel does not cost less than an orange from Spain) and if European producers have to bring down their prices to be competitive on a number of foreign markets, they will get equivalent compensation so that they don't lose out and are not discouraged from exporting. This is the system the Americans are always complaining about during GATT negotiations; the emergence of Eastern European agriculture is not making the situation any easier and the Community is loath to rush into drastic changes until the air clears a bit.

All this naturally places a strain on the EC budget and it means money that does not go into research, health, education, etc. The need to reform the CAP is obvious and has been accepted by everyone. Already certain measures have been taken, such as imposing production quotas, setting guarantee thresholds above which the producer finances all or part of the extra cost, giving compensation for letting land lie fallow, etc. At the same time it is also becoming clearer and clearer that the social cost of letting growing numbers of people abandon farming is becoming exorbitant, in terms of unemployment, urban violence, etc. All these elements had to be taken into account in trying to find a global solution. This rather terrifying job was put into the hands of the European Commissioner in charge of agriculture, Ray

MacSharry. In July 1989, Mr MacSharry submitted his project to the European Parliament and the Council of Ministers. If it goes through – but that is somewhat wishful thinking – the new measures would start being implemented in 1993 and be totally operational by 1996.

Amongst these measures are:

– a significant decrease in prices (– 35% for cereals, – 10% for milk, – 15% for butter, – 15% for beef);

– a stricter production control through stronger quotas, in particular on milk and tobacco, limits on subsidies to sheep breeders, 'freezing' cereal–producing land, etc.;

– compensation for all this through subsidies in favour of extensive breeding of good quality cattle;

– improving the system of direct aid to small and medium-sized farms, producing cereals on less than 50 acres of land or less than 200,000 kg of milk a year. Subsidies would also depend on methods of production and would be more favourable to farmers who take precautions against ruining the environment.

All in all, what the MacSharry project is promoting is a policy in favour of the smaller farmers through a different distribution of subsidies, in favour of more 'ecological' farming (obviously, as things stand, this kind of farming is more expensive than extensive agriculture using nitrates by the ton and feeding cattle on cheap soya instead of cereals, but, if subsidies are going to be given out anyway, is it not preferable to subsidize natural products and environment-conscious farmers rather than wine lakes and butter mountains?); the project also promotes reforestation and a policy of price curbs that should be beneficial to the consumer and might also entice him to buy a bit more of certain products.

All this, however, is not making the bigger farmers very happy, and they are being pretty vocal about it. This has been most obvious in France – demonstrations have lately appeared to be particularly well orchestrated, with political objectives and carefully thought-out outbreaks of violence, with the very real plight of the small farmer being used as a rather effective smokescreen.

Fisheries

Europe's 300,000 fishermen catch some 7 million tons of fish per year – this represents 7.2% of the world total and puts the Europeans fourth in line behind Japan, the Soviet Union and

China. Even though the actual number of fishermen is relatively limited, there are in fact four or five times that many people whose work depends on the fishing industry, whether it's ship-building, food-processing, etc. Fish has enjoyed (in a manner of speaking) an ever-growing popularity with European consumers in the last fifty years.

The EC fisheries policy does, however, have to face problems that are exactly the opposite to those that beset agriculture; in other words, too much demand for not enough home production, with the ever-present threat of seeing the coastal seas of Europe emptied of their fish. Then what?

There are two important dates in the history of European fisheries policy. Even though a common policy was announced in the Treaty of Rome, nobody actually did anything much until 1970. That year, the Council of Ministers set out the main rules governing equal access to fishing zones in EC waters; they created a common fishing organization with the ad hoc mechanisms to support prices and protect the EC market so as to allow a rational development of fishing activities, a decent standard of living for the fishermen, stabilize the market and ensure proper supplies at affordable prices for the consumer. The Community was also charged with coordinating national policies and supplementing them when necessary with its own financial aid, so as to ensure more equitable conditions of competition.

Second important date: 1983. The fisheries policy took on a new dimension with a whole series of measures aimed at preserving fishing zones. This had become necessary because in the 'seventies a number of countries decided to extend their exclusive fishing zones to 200 miles from their coasts (it was the time of the Great Cod War between Britain and Iceland). By 1977, it had become obvious that the Community would have to do the same, if only because whole fishing armadas excluded from the new, enlarged zones were coming into its waters, with the ensuing threat of disastrous decreases in the fish population. (It was the time of intermittent guerrilla warfare between French and Spanish fishermen.) This 200-mile limit is therefore in force in the Atlantic; it has not been possible to impose it in the Mediterranean, as it would mean encroaching on other, non-EC countries' fishing zones. This has meant, however, determining quotas for each country and each category of fish. They are known as TACs (Total Authorized Captures).

From 1977 to 1983, a long process of internal negotiations had to be pursued for the Community to be entrusted with the responsibility for all fishing resources. It all came together in January 1983.

Then, the Community had to negotiate bilateral agreements with outside countries who wished to continue fishing in EC waters, so that its fishermen would get the same rights in those countries' waters.

Normally, the principle of non-discrimination between EC member States (one of the basic principles of the Treaty of Rome) means that EC fishermen can cast their nets freely in all Community waters. However, there are exceptions, would you believe. Since 1973, Denmark, Ireland and the United Kingdom benefit from a special clause which allows them to keep for their own exclusive use a twelve-mile fishing zone along their coasts.

2. Regional policies

Fact: although the European Community as a whole undoubtedly ranks amongst the richest areas of the world, within its borders there are enormous differences in the levels of development and prosperity.

Consequently, one of the objectives of Community institutions must be to try to redistribute this wealth a bit more equitably by encouraging economic development in every field of activity in those areas that are most underprivileged.

There are on the whole two main types of 'poorer' regions in the EC.

– There are the ones that suffer, and have long suffered, from lack of industrial activity and economic progress. They are mainly situated along the outer edges of the EC (Ireland, Greece, Southern Italy, Southern Spain, etc.). These areas suffer from insufficient infrastructures (transport, roads, power supplies, etc.), a relatively low standard of living and relatively high levels of unemployment. Agriculture remains a major element in their economy.

– Then there are those areas that have known prosperity but whose economy has declined because their industrial base is crumbling. They are officially considered as being 'in the process of redevelopment'. Every European country has one or several of these areas (Wallonia in Belgium, Lorraine and Nord-Pas de

Calais in France, the Welsh mining valleys and the Midlands in Britain, the Ruhr in Germany if we exclude the ex-DDR) where mostly steel, coal and textile industries have gone through a severe crisis.

A lot of Community effort has gone into trying to help all these areas, in particular since the petrol crises of the early 'seventies, but the prosperity gap has just got wider and wider. And today, when economic difficulties are back again for everyone, the less prosperous zones face the dire prospect of getting poorer and poorer while the richer zones, although they won't be getting much richer, are going to look like Paradise compared to the rest – the consequence being a threat of 'internal emigration' that would lead to severe demographic and social dysfunction.

It was therefore vital that the Single Market – which is hopefully destined to increase the EC's global prosperity – should avoid exacerbating these differences by giving a major impulse to the richer regions while making the struggle even more difficult for the others. This is why the Community authorities decided in 1988 to give a strong boost to the various development funds, by improving their financial means and increasing their efficiency.

As we already know, (see page 62) these Funds can now contribute financially to specific projects *before* they get off the ground, instead of coming along afterwards to reimburse expenses already made which meant that projects had to be already put in motion before obtaining preliminary financing – very logical.

What the Community has done is to coordinate as much as possible the objectives and the actions of the various Funds so that there is no undue overlapping or, on the contrary, areas of no man's land where projects slip through the financial net.

Basically, there are five main objectives:
– helping the structural adjustment of underdeveloped areas (like Belfast, in Northern Ireland);
– helping redevelop areas affected by industrial decline (these two objectives can be pursued mostly by the European Regional Development Fund, or ERDF, and partly by the European Social Fund, or ESF);
– fighting long-term unemployment;
– helping vocational training and professional integration of young people;

– speeding up the modernization of agricultural structures and promoting the development of rural areas. (The body responsible for this is the European Agricultural Guidance and Guarantee Fund.)

Complementary financial help for all these objectives can be sought through the European Investment Bank.

What are the main criteria governing the allocation of funds?

The first one concerns those regions where gross domestic product (GDP) is less than three-quarters of the Community average, over a period of three years.

The second criterion concerns areas where the rate of unemployment has been higher than the Community average for more than three years, where the ratio of people working in industry compared to the total working population is equal to or higher than the Community average and where industrial employment is officially declining.

These same criteria apply to regions where agriculture is still the main source of income, with an additional aspect: how near they are to the periphery of the Community.

This action through Community funds complements national programmes or contributes to them. It is achieved by the European Commission, the member State directly involved and the competent authorities at the required level (regional, local, etc.), all working together at preparing, financing, implementing and then assessing the whole operation.

CAR TELEPHONES: THE EUROPEAN LINE

More than 3.5 million Europeans use car telephones; 1.2 million are British. But can all these people use the same car telephone system throughout Europe? Yes, if they are connected to the European car telephone system that has been in operation since the beginning of 1992 and is known as GSM (Global System for Mobile Communications). This very sophisticated digital system is not limited by radio frequencies, which are often different from one European country to another. Now it will be possible to use the same car phone throughout seventeen European countries. The system (which is 20 to 40% cheaper than the traditional one) is now attracting a lot of interest in countries like Japan and New Zealand.

12 What now?

EAST WIND, WEST WIND . . .

Since that memorable night in November 1989 when the Berlin Wall came tumbling down, with a bit of help from its erstwhile victims, the concept of a United Europe has taken on a whole new dimension.

De Gaulle's vision of one Europe 'de l'Atlantique à l'Oural' is becoming less and less of a vision, more and more of a perspective – and that means taking practical decisions, shifting structures, signing agreements, setting deadlines. It also means a lot of worried people.

Euphoria at seeing totalitarian regimes crumbling in quick succession was swiftly replaced by perplexity and even anxiety. Western Europe was like a man who has spent a great deal of time leaning against a solidly shut door that suddenly swings open: he's having to do some pretty nifty footwork if he wants to keep his balance and not fall head over heels into the unknown. When the Iron Curtain flew open, Europe was in grave danger of losing its balance, and the European Community even more so.

It would be hypocritical to deny that at the time when the Common Market was created, European leaders were spurred on towards some form of unity partly by the threatening presence of the Communist bloc in the East. As time passed and the European Community shaped its own identity, we all tended to forget to what extent a nice, visible, solid threat to the East represented a sort of common punchbag that kept everybody hitting out in the same direction rather than at one another. When that threat suddenly fell apart, Western Europeans were left staring at each other in wild surmise.

It got even worse when, practically immediately, we found ourselves confronted with an explosion of nationalistic separatisms and a global economic and social disaster area. At that point, many began to wonder if it had been a good idea to have spent so much time and money on propaganda for our capitalist paradise; as long as a few dozen or maybe even a few hundred refugees from Eastern Europe arrived on our shores along the years, we could afford to welcome them with more or less open arms. But millions of them? There was no way Western economies could withstand the shock. So the best solution for all concerned was to encourage Eastern Europeans to stay at home by helping them rebuild their own economies on the same lines as ours.

There was, however, one EC member State who was not, at that stage, suffering from any qualms about the opening to the East, and that, of course, was West Germany. From the moment the Berlin Wall came down, the march towards a united Germany was as rapid as it was inexorable.

Not that it did anything towards soothing the fears of the other Europeans. There is no denying that the perspective of an 80-million-strong German State looming over the European Community was not everybody's idea of an ideal future. But the alternative was even less encouraging: trying to stop East and West Germany from uniting would not only be totally ineffective but would undoubtedly result in a serious rift between the Germans and the rest of the Community. And that might encourage Germany to gather round it as many Eastern States as possible and forge a separate economic – and political – bloc which would, given time, become a formidable competitor for Western Europe.

That wily French statesman and diplomat, Charles Maurice de Talleyrand, once said: 'Il vaut mieux favoriser ce que l'on n'est pas en mesure d'empêcher', which best translates in English as 'If you can't beat 'em, join 'em'. Jacques Delors may have had both formulas in mind when in January 1990, before the European Parliament, he indicated that, in his opinion, East Germany should be given special treatment and be allowed to join the Community before 1992. This suggestion was not greeted with unanimous approval by the Twelve. Quite a few European leaders were worried at the state of the East German economy and feared that its entry into the European monetary system would destabilize the whole financial structure of the Community. Chancellor Helmut Köhl set about persuading them that German unity would not have an adverse effect on the Community or the Single Market and that, in any case, West Germany was willing and able to bear the brunt of the East German reconstruction. He was helped by Mikhail Gorbachev, the Soviet president, who put no obstacle in the way of German unification, even if it meant Eastern Germany becoming a member of NATO.

So, a specially convened European summit, on 28 April 1990 in Dublin, ended by giving its seal of approval to the principle of German unity and by underlying the importance for the Community of being involved in the whole process from the start. The East Germans having voted to become part of the Federal Republic of Germany, the EC was not, therefore, going from a twelve-State to a thirteen-State community. A careful study of the legal, technical and commercial situation revealed the fact that some 80% of EC regulations could be applied, as they stood, to the five new Länder of Germany.

For the rest – which concerned essentially commercial links with the COMECON (the Eastern European and Soviet economic body), agriculture and the environment – the Community did what it had done for several of its more recent members: it allowed for a period of transition, until the end of 1992 for agriculture, of 1995 for the environment (except for nuclear sites, which were required to be adapted without delay to EC security norms). As for COMECON, it fell apart practically of its own volition.

It was estimated that the process of integrating Eastern Germany into the EC would cost the Community some 500 million ECUs a year until 1993. The EC's swift involvement in the German unification has meant that investments in the new Länder are not the sole prerogative of the West Germans, even though they are well in the lead, as is only natural. According to a report published by the Treubendanstalt (the body responsible for privatizations), by August 1991, barely a year after unification, a third of the nine thousand State companies had been totally or partly bought by German or foreign investors; 156 companies went to non-German buyers, starting with the French (47), followed by the Swiss (22), the Dutch (20), the Belgians (18), the Swedes (17) and the Austrians (13).

Another anxiety Chancellor Köhl has been keen to allay is that Germany would be too immersed in the problems of unification to really bother about the Single Act or the advance towards monetary union. On the contrary, Germany never faltered in its support of both concepts.

What was done for East Germany without too much wailing and gnashing of teeth could not, however, be done for the other Eastern European States.

To start with, there was no reason why they shouldn't take their place in the queue. Other countries in Western Europe, like Austria or Sweden, have put down their names for membership of the EC and it would be totally unfair to give others priority over them, Prodigal Son or no Prodigal Son. Secondly, it was quite obvious that these countries emerging from forty years of collectivism and struggling in the throes of dire economic problems, would never have been able to stand the strain of keeping up with Community standards in every field of endeavour. They just didn't have the infrastructure. However, that did not imply turning the EC into some sort of 'fortress Europe' while the rest of the continent sorted itself out as best it could. Even before the fall of the Berlin Wall, during the celebrations of the French Revolution Bicentenary in July 1989, the leaders of the world's more industrialized countries, meeting at La Grande Arche in Paris, officially entrusted to the European Commission the task of coordinating assistance to Eastern European States. This assistance was not limited to the members of the European Community – it actually involved the twenty-four countries belonging to the OECD (Organization of Economic Cooperation and Development). The idea was to ensure coherence in the financial aid extended to Eastern Europe. Otherwise, there would have been a risk of money being spent to the advantage of one or two countries and the detriment of others, or priority being constantly given to certain sectors of the economy which were maybe in less difficulty than others.

As for the Community as such, it had to organize its own contributions. The first step was to set up a programme, code-named **PHARE**, aimed at financing reconstruction by means of three types of initiative: 'lending' Western experts where technical assistance and know-how were needed, providing goods and materials where necessary, advancing starting-off funds; this in all the fields of activity that urgently needed restructuring, be it agriculture, energy, trade, services, vocational training, etc. PHARE started out in 1990 with a fund of 500,000 ECUs, which was doubled in 1991. The first two countries involved were Hungary and Poland, followed in swift succession by Bulgaria, Czechoslovakia, Romania and Yugoslavia. As for Albania, in 1991 it was allocated emergency humanitarian and medical aid of several million ECUs, plus shipments of 150,000 tons of wheat.

Also in 1990, the twelve Heads of State and government, meeting in November in Paris, agreed to set up a bank specially geared to helping Eastern European countries. The European Bank of Reconstruction and Development, known as BERD (from its French title, Banque Européenne de Reconstruction et de Développement), was set up in London. From 1989 to 1991, the twenty-four OECD countries spent some 23 billion ECUs in help to Eastern Europe – 14 billion in straight donations, 9 billion in loans.

On top of that, the European Community extended to the Soviet Union (as it still was at the time) some 750 million ECUs in emergency aid, although the USSR was not involved in the PHARE programme.

But it isn't simply a question of pouring money into the Eastern economies. For instance, within the PHARE programme is another one, code-named **TEMPUS** (Trans European Mobility Programme for University Studies) which, since 1990, coordinates links between universities and businesses involved in Eastern European reconstruction. All Eastern European countries are involved, including Albania and the Baltic Republics. An important part of the programme, which is financed through the PHARE structure, is concerned with engineering and business management. It also allocated grants to students and teachers. By October 1991, the British were already involved in some 98 of the TEMPUS projects (against 52 for the French). According to David O'Sullivan, Head of Division at the European Commission's Human Resources Task Force, TEMPUS is not affected by the political or social upheavals some of the Eastern European countries are suffering from, because projects are dealt with directly by universities, businesses and/or organizations, not by governments.

On a more general level, however, it's obviously easier for the Community to deal with those countries that have managed to establish the structures of a true democratic system. This is especially the case for Czechoslovakia, Hungary and Poland. The result was that, in November 1991, those three countries all signed association agreements with the EC that went well beyond simple economic and commercial cooperation. These agreements specifically state that the final objective of the three countries is to become members of the European Community. There is no date set for this future membership; it's all going to depend on the rate of these countries' economic and social development. They do however envisage a time-limit of ten years for setting up, at the very least, a free-trade zone for industrial products.

The agreements also stipulate that the EC will open its own borders to Eastern European products faster than those countries will to Community products. Not that it's going to be all plain sailing, far from it. What Eastern European countries have got to sell at the moment are mainly agricultural products.

Which is definitely NOT what the EC needs. Difficulties have already cropped up, for instance on the question of East European beef being sold in the EC at bargain prices, which has angered Community farmers, especially the French (and everybody knows what happens to products, alive or dead, that French farmers disapprove of . . .). A temporary solution was worked out, by the expedient of buying Eastern European meat, not for EC consumption, but to send to the Soviets in the form of alimentary aid.

So, from a purely economic viewpoint, the European Community got its act together without too much kerfuffle. Unfortunately, most of this effort went completely unnoticed by the majority of Europeans, whose attention was focused on two major political upheavals: the Gulf War to start with, followed by the civil war in Yugoslavia, all in the same year of 1991. In both cases, the European Community found itself being violently criticized for not being what it wasn't geared up to be in the first place: a political power. So, the Heads of State and government who got together in the Dutch town of Maastricht in December 1991 to discuss the next steps towards a future single currency, were quick to realize that it wouldn't be enough. What the Europeans, and the rest of the world, were expecting from them, were the ways and means of giving the EC more political clout.

FROM EUROPEAN COMMUNITY
TO EUROPEAN UNION

The unification of Germany was, to all intents and purposes, a political act. Consequently, accepting East Germany into the European Community as part of the new German entity was, fundamentally, and whichever way you want to look at it, a political decision. Obviously, the arguments for or against were always couched in economic terms, as befits an economic body such as the EC; but the very fact that the subject being discussed was Germany – divided as a result of its own appalling responsibilities in the Second World War, and, what is more, divided into two intrinsically incompatible regimes – meant that the Twelve were faced with a weighty political decision. Yet when, at the Dublin summit, they all voted in favour of German unity, the political impact of such a decision did not seem to attract a great deal of attention. Why? Because, as is often the case with the Community, public opinion can't see the political wood for the economic trees; the political issues are often put aside or under wraps even on an official level, for the simple reason that most economic decisions would never be taken if their political consequences were being constantly dragged into the discussions.

With the Gulf War, it was exactly the opposite. Everybody was so busy bemoaning the lack of political unity within the Community, that very few people paid any attention to the fact that Europeans were spared the spiralling petrol prices of the 'seventies due to the conflict between Israel and the Arab States. European economic unity, the practical mechanisms of EC solidarity turned out to be very useful, whereas in the preceding crises it had been every man for himself, at least to start with. But the Community's capacity for economic self-preservation was not a sufficient argument in the eyes of the Europeans. The fact that everybody took it for granted was proof already that the EC had reached a distinct level of efficiency; but it was also proof that even more was being demanded of it, not only from its own citizens but from the world outside. Of course, all the Community leaders were unanimous in denouncing the invasion of Kuwait by Iraq, but then, so did the vast majority of countries throughout the world. What was galling for the Europeans was that a) the EC as such had no say in the decision to wage war against Iraq and b) even if it had been consulted, it would have been incapable of taking a common stand. Each individual country took its own decision, according to its own situation – the UK flew to the help of the USA without even a backward glance at its eleven partners; France, with grave misgivings and after having made sure that no diplomatic stone had been left unturned, also joined the American armed camp; Germany, plunged into its unification process, contributed financially, but not militarily, and so on . . . The European Community, everybody kept repeating, was an economic giant, but a political dwarf – conveniently forgetting that no EC structure had yet been prepared with the aim of turning it into a political giant. It had no common defence system, no common army, no common foreign policy, not even a common position on a possible future political structure. In other words, there was nothing that enabled the European Community to take a straight political decision, as opposed to an economic decision with political implications.

Nobody paid any attention to the fact that the Community had decided on economic sanctions against Iraq even before the United Nations' embargo was voted; nor that the European involvement in the resulting blockade was coordinated by the Western European Union – the intergovernmental organization in charge of promoting cooperation between seven EC States in matters of defence, in collaboration with NATO. It was already too late for all that – Iraq most obviously snubbed any EC diplomatic initiative and did its best to divide the member States between themselves, particularly by linking the fate of the Western hostages to the attitude of their home countries. It didn't succeed in the sense that they all agreed on principle to condemn Iraq, but they certainly didn't all face the actual fact of war in the same way.

This lack of political coherence and clout did not show any sign of improving when the Community had to face the civil war in Yugoslavia at the end of 1991. In all justice, between the end of one conflict and the beginning of the next, plus, in the middle, the attempted putsch in Moscow, the EC would never have had the time to set up a unifying structure. However, the Twelve did, to the best of their ability, present a united front, although that front concealed different national attitudes to the conflict, with the Germans maintaining a historical solidarity with the Croats, while the French remembered their links with the Serbs and the British, mindful of their own experience in Northern

Ireland, were totally opposed to any intervention other than diplomatic. The Community, nevertheless, made a concerted effort to try and stop the fighting between Serbs and Croats – their official negotiator, Lord Carrington, was not faced with the humiliation of being ignored, but none of the many cease-fire agreements he persuaded the Yugoslavs to sign was respected. The economic sanctions decided on by the Community had no effect whatsoever. The Twelve were accused of having ignored the danger signals that had for months preceded the actual fighting (as if, during those months, the whole world hadn't had its attention focused on the Gulf), and, once fighting had broken out, of not being capable of taking definitive action, like recognizing Croatian independence or making the Serbs respect the existing borders of Croatia. The United Nations eventually obtained an effective ceasefire, while the European Community was proving to be unable to solve conflicts on its own doorstep, never mind the Middle East.

And yet, behind the scenes, the Europeans were steadily working to try and strengthen the unity of the EC not only economically but politically as well. In December 1990, the Heads of State and government (in other words the European Council), meeting in Rome, set up two intergovernmental teams, including, as that implies, representatives from the various governments, not from the European Institutions, to work on monetary and political union respectively. The result, a year later, was the Maastricht summit, which officially started the Community on the road towards the single currency and the beginnings of a political union. Easier said than done. During the months preceding the 9 and 10 December meetings in Maastricht, disagreement was rife between the Twelve and not only because of the conflicts breaking out here and there. The UK government, in particular, declared itself totally hostile to practically everything that was being suggested, including the single currency, any kind of political agreement that might lead to 'federalism' and any kind of social convention (too expensive . . .). It looked as if a stalemate had been reached, especially as Germany wouldn't hear of 'sacrificing' the Deutschmark to a common currency, namely the ECU, without any social counterpart. But the Netherlands, who were chairing the Community for the second half of 1991, came up with what became known as 'the opt-out clause', which allowed the UK to put the question of adopting the single currency before its national Parliament a second time, prior to the ECU becoming once and for all the European coinage. The British were not too keen at being thus singled out and tried to get the opt-out clause included in the final agreement as a general option for all concerned, but this was not accepted.

At the Maastricht summit, the Twelve started out by agreeing that the advance towards monetary union would officially be declared 'irreversible'. So there was no turning back for anybody, except for the British, who know perfectly well however that, should they be the only ones to refuse the single European currency at the last minute, they would in fact be placing themselves beyond the Community pale. But in any case, there's no need yet to go that far; a certain number of conditions will have to be met before any member State can join the 'ECU club': reduced inflation, reduced long-term interest rates, a budgetary deficit equal to no more than 3% of Gross Domestic Product, public debt no higher than 6% of GDP, a minimum two-year history of exchange rate stability within the European Monetary System. The 'irreversible' aspect of monetary union was emphasized by the decision to set specific dates for establishing the single currency.

The Twelve also agreed that submitting political decisions to the systematic need for a unanimous vote of approval was resulting in no decision being taken at all. So it was established that the European Council would be responsible for deciding which major foreign policy questions could, to start with, be subjected to a common vote at Community, rather than national, level. Then they would decide – unanimously – which aspects of these questions could be subjected to a qualified majority vote, so as to avoid stalemate through the veto of a single member. A slow, rather top-heavy procedure, but at least it was the first step towards moving out of the cul-de-sac of unanimous votes and possible vetoes.

Simultaneously, it was decided that the Western European Union would be put in charge of elaborating a common defence policy – complementing the already existing NATO alliance (and not submitted to NATO, as some hoped and others feared). WEU would be given more operational powers from which, eventually, a common European defence force would spring.

Finally, faced with the UK's bitter opposition, the other European leaders decided that the Social Charter (see page 63) would not be made an integral part of the future 'Treaty of the

Union' everyone was working up to, but would constitute a sort of appendix or annexe, which would avoid the UK having to sign it; however, for the eleven countries who have already adopted it, the Charter would from now on contain certain aspects that could be applied by a qualified majority rather than unanimously (namely the clauses concerning better working conditions and equal rights for women at work).

All in all, where is the Maastricht agreement leading the Community? Apparently to becoming a European Union, but the question is: how? A careful scrutiny of the terms of the agreement does enable the reader to establish a timetable of sorts.

From December 1991 to 1 January 1993 (when the Single Market is officially born): the decisions taken at Maastricht are put into the proper legal form and submitted to the national Parliaments (or to a referendum) in all twelve States for ratification. They then become a treaty. In the meantime, the final measures of the Single Act yet to be agreed upon must be adopted.

Another move towards the abolition of border control will be the creation of a European police organization known as EUROPOL, along the lines of Interpol, but for the Community alone. Its first task will be to coordinate police action in the matter of drugs traffic.

The various member States will have to start putting their financial houses in order if they want to be able, eventually, to meet the conditions necessary for joining the monetary union.

On the defence front, other EC countries are going to have to join the Western European Union, so that work can start on preparing a common defence policy. The first to join may be Greece. Ireland will have to decide what it intends to do about its official position as a neutral country.

From 1993 to 1996, the measures contained in the Single Act will be applied in the field, one after the other. Borders will be abolished, starting with the ones between countries who signed the Schengen Convention (see page 148). According to the terms of the Maastricht agreement, the citizens of the Community living in an EC country other than their own will be given the right to vote and to be elected at local and European elections in their country of residence.

In January 1994, a European Monetary Institute will be set up. Its job will be to prepare the structures of the future European Central Bank that will replace the national Banks (Bundesbank,

Banque de France, etc.) when the ECU becomes the single currency. In June that same year, European elections will be organized – normally according to the same voting procedure throughout the EC. In Maastricht, the European Parliament was given slightly more powers (though not as many as it wished), in particular that of approving or not the nomination of new Commissioners.

In 1995, Austria and Sweden, who have applied for membership, should be admitted into the Community.

From 1996 to 1999 will be the time when the decisive steps towards monetary union are taken.

At the end of 1996, the Twelve – or Fourteen – will get together to examine the financial situation of each country: if seven of these countries fulfil the economic and financial conditions set by the Maastricht summit, the European Council will need a two-thirds majority vote to set up a European Central Bank and a single currency. If the two-thirds majority is not obtained, or if there are not seven 'healthy' countries, the European Central Bank will be automatically created a bit later, in July 1998, and the single currency will automatically come into existence on 1 January 1999, at least for those countries that are then financially healthy, whether they like it or not. As for the UK, it will have to decide at that point, once and for all, what its attitude is going to be.

After 1999: it's anybody's guess!

Naturally, as with all forecasts, this scenario is conditioned by future events. If it works out, it will mean that no catastrophe has cropped up to delay or halt the Union. It is also rather simplified, in the sense that other important decisions will certainly be taken, concerning foreign policy, defence, social protection, environment, culture, consumer protection, etc. Other countries may ask to join – there's talk of Finland, Norway, Turkey, and even Switzerland . . .

Come what may, we can be sure of one thing: in the months and years to come, we may be worried Europeans, angry Europeans, enthusiastic Europeans and, why not, even happy Europeans, but we most certainly won't be . . . bored Europeans!

Eurospeak

ARION
EC programme financing study trips for teachers in the various Community countries.

BABEL
Fund for the dubbing and subtitling, in the different EC languages, of European films and telefilms.

BERD
Banque Européenne pour la Reconstruction et le Développement. European Bank for Reconstruction and Development. Community banking institution specializing in financial help to Eastern European countries.

BRITE
Basic Research on Industrial Technologies for Europe. Programme for the application of new technology to traditional industries.

CAP
Common Agricultural Policy.

CEDEFOP
Centre Européen pour le Développement de la Formation Professionnelle. Organization for the development and promotion of vocational training in the EC.

COMETT
Community in Education and Training for Technology. Programme for the promotion of regular links between businesses and higher education establishments doing advanced technology courses.

COREPER
Comité des Représentants Permanents des Etats Membres des Communautés Européennes. Committee of Permanent Representatives of Member States. Group of the Permanent Representatives (Ambassadors) of the Twelve, and their Aides; acts as liaison between the European Commission and the European Council of Ministers.

COUNCIL OF EUROPE
Intergovernmental organization for social, cultural, judicial and political cooperation between European States who recognize the Rights of Man.

COURT OF JUSTICE
Judicial institution based in Luxembourg; makes sure that European legislation is properly respected and that this legislation, in its turn, is not prejudicial to any EC citizen or organization.

COURT FOR THE RIGHTS OF MAN
Judicial institution based in Strasbourg; makes sure that no national rule, law or initiative is contrary to the European Convention on the Rights of Man.

DELTA
Programme to help develop computerized equipment for teachers.

DIRECTIVE
Community text obliging all member States to conform their national law, on a specific question, to Community law, usually within a two-year period.

EAGGF
European Agricultural Guidance and Guarantee Fund.

ECSC
European Coal and Steel Community.

ECU
European Currency Unit.

EFTA
European Free Trade Association.

EHLASS
European Home and Leisure Accident Surveillance System.

EIB
European Investment Bank.

EMS
European Monetary System.

ENVIREG
Programme organizing the fight against pollution in coastal areas.

ERASMUS
European Action Scheme for the Mobility of University Students. Programme to help students and teachers pursue a period of study in another EC country.

ERDF
European Regional Development Fund.

ERM
Exchange Rate Mechanism.

ESF
European Social Fund.

ESPRIT
European Strategic Programme for Information Technologies.

EUCREA
Organization linking national bodies involved in stimulating artistic creativity amongst the disabled.

EURATOM
European Atomic Energy Community.

EURO-AIM
EC network promoting commercialization of European TV productions.

EUROCOOP
European Community of Consumer Cooperatives.

EUROPEAN COMMISSION
Seventeen-member executive body of the European Community; based in Brussels.

EUROPEAN COUNCIL
Twice-yearly summit of the EC Heads of State and government.

EUROPEAN COUNCIL OF MINISTERS
EC institution uniting the Ministers responsible for a particular subject. Votes on all the EC directives.

EUROPOL
Future European police organization, aimed primarily at co-ordinating the struggle against drugs traffic.

EUROS
Eventual symbol of a possible European shipping fleet.

EUROTECNET
European Technology Network. Programme stimulating exchanges and research on new technology in vocational training.

EURYDICE
Information network on education in the European Community. Database system.

EUTELSAT
European Telecommunications Satellite Organization.

GATT
General Agreement on Tariffs and Trade. Multilateral treaty aimed at facilitating and coordinating international trade exchanges.

HANDYNET
Computerized information system covering all questions concerning the disabled in the EC.

HELIOS
Community programme for the disabled.

HORIZON
Aid programme financing vocational training for handi-capped people.

IRIS

EC network of vocational training programmes for women.

JET

Joint European Torus. Experimental installation of controlled thermonuclear fusion, set up in Culham (UK).

LINGUA

EC programme to help young people learn a second Community language.

LOME CONVENTION

Agreement signed and reviewed between the EC and sixty-six African, Caribbean and Pacific countries by which the Community undertakes to finance various development projects in those countries.

MATTHAEUS

EC programme aimed at helping customs officers coordinate their actions at a Community level.

MEDIA

Programme to stimulate and promote European film and TV production throughout the Community.

MEDSPA

Anti-pollution programme to protect the Mediterranean inside and outside Community borders.

MEP

Member of the European Parliament.

PETRA

Programme Européen pour le Travail des Adultes. EC programme to help vocational training projects for 16-to 25-year-olds.

PHARE

EC programme aimed at helping economic reconstruction in Eastern Europe.

RACE

Research and Development in Advanced Communications Technology in Europe. Programme for the development of future telecommunications networks.

REGULATION
Major decision taken by the Commission and the Council of Ministers, directly applicable in every EC State, without going through national authorities.

SCHENGEN CONVENTION
Agreement on free circulation of citizens across borders, signed and ratified by eight EC member States.

SINGLE ACT
Treaty signed in 1986, modifying the original Treaty of Rome in order to achieve an effective Single Market and a European Union by 1 January 1993.

SOCIAL CHARTER
Signed by eleven out of twelve states. Lays down the fundamental principles of a European social policy.

STEP
Science and Technology for Environment and Protection. Programme for developing methods of protecting human health against environmental pollution.

TAC
Total Admissible Captures. Maximum quotas on certain categories of fish caught in EC waters.

TIDE
Technology for the Integration of the Disabled and Elderly.

YOUTH EXCHANGE PROGRAMME
Promotes cultural exchanges between groups of young people belonging to the different EC countries.

Addresses

GENERAL

British Standards Institution
2 Park Street
London W1A 2BS
Tel: 071 629 9000

CEDEFOP
Bundesallee 22
D-1000 Berlin 15
GERMANY

Department of Trade and Industry (DTI)
The Single Market Unit
Room 42
1-9 Victoria Street
London SW1H 0ET
Tel: 081 200 1992

European Commission
200 Rue de la Loi
B-1049 Brussels
BELGIUM

European Commission–London Office
Jean Monnet House
8 Storey's Gate
London SW1P 3AT
Tel: 071 973 1992

European Investment Bank
68 Pall Mall
London SW1Y 5ES
Tel: 071 839 3351

European Parliament
Information Office
2 Queen Anne's Gate
London SW1H 9AA
Tel: 071 222 0411

Health and Safety Commission
Old Marylebone Road
London NW1
Tel: 071 229 3456

HM Customs and Excise
Griffin House
161 Hammersmith Road
London W6 8BL
Tel: 081 748 8010
or The Collector of Customs and
Excise at port or airport of arrival,
for overseas residents

THE ENVIRONMENT

Royal Commission on Environmental Pollution
Church House
Great Smith Street
London SW1P 3BL
Tel: 071 212 8620

Department of the Environment (DoE)
2 Marsham Street
London SW1P 3EB
Tel: 071 276 3000

European Foundation for the Improvement of Living and Working Conditions
Loughlinstown House
Shanklin
County Dublin
REPUBLIC OF IRELAND

HEALTH ABROAD

DSS Overseas Branch
OVB–BGE (EC)
Newcastle-upon-Tyne NE98 1YX
Tel: 091 213 5000

MEDICINE

The Home Office Drugs Branch
50 Queen Anne's Gate
London SW1H 9AT

SOCIAL SECURITY BENEFITS AND PENSIONS

Department of Social Security
Overseas Branch
Newcastle-upon-Tyne NE98 1YX

WOMEN'S RIGHTS

The Commission of the European Communities
Directorate General 5 (Bureau for questions concerning employment and equal treatment for women)
200 Rue de la Loi
B-1049 Brussels
BELGIUM

Equal Opportunities Commission
Overseas House
Quay Street
Manchester M3 3HN
Tel: 061 833 9244

YOUTH AND EDUCATION

ARION
Padagogischer Austauschdienst
Nassestrasse 8
D-5300 Bonn 1
GERMANY

COMETT Liaison Office
Room 6/17, Elizabeth House
York Road
London SE1 7PH

ERASMUS
UK Erasmus Student Grants Council
The University of Kent
Canterbury
Kent CT2 7PD
Tel: 0227 762712

Paul Finet Foundation
JMO/C4/26A
Jean Monnet Building
Plateau du Kirchberg
Luxembourg

IRIS
CREW–38 rue Stevin
B-1040 Brussels
BELGIUM

Jean Monnet Fellowships
Academic Service
European University Institute
CP No. 2355
1-50100 Firenze Ferrovia
ITALY

Jean Monnet Project
University Information–DG X (ten)
Commission of the European Communities
200 Rue de la Loi
B-1049 Brussels
BELGIUM

PETRA
Department of Employment
Caxton House
Tothill Street
London SW1
Tel: 071 273 5397

Robert Schuman Scholarships
Directorate General for Research and Documentation
The European Parliament–Bâtiment R. Schuman
Plateau de Kirchberg
Luxembourg
or
UK Office of the European Parliament
2 Queen Anne's Gate
London SW1H 9AA

UK LINGUA Unit
Strand 4,
Seymour Mews House
Seymour Mews
London W1H 9PE

Youth Exchange Centre & Young Workers Exchange Programme
Seymour Mews House
Seymour Mews
London W1H 9PE
Tel: 071 486 5101

Euro Info Centres

Euro Info Centres provide an information and advice service of direct use to professionals and businessmen. Most questions relate to Community policies and programmes, instruments for business, finance and company law. Through cooperation with other Centres in the Community, EICs are able to supply details on national legislation and business practices in other member States.

There are presently 21 EICs in the United Kingdom, 187 throughout the Community.

Local Enterprise Development Unit
LEDU House
Upper Galwally
Belfast BT8 4TB
Tel: 0232 491031

Birmingham Chamber of Industry and Commerce
75 Harbone Road
PO Box 360
Birmingham B15 3DH
Tel: 021 455 0268

Federation of Sussex Industries and Chamber of Commerce
Seven Dials
Brighton BN1 3JS
Tel: 0273 26282/5

Bristol Chamber of Commerce and Industry
16 Clifton Park
Bristol BS8 3BY
Tel: 0272 737373

Exeter Enterprise Ltd
University of Exeter
Hailey Wing, Reed Hall
Exeter EX4 4QR
Tel: 0392 214085

Scottish Development Agency
Euro Info Centre
21 Bothwell Street
Glasgow G2 6NR
Tel: 041 221 0999

Highland Opportunity Ltd
Development Department
Highland Regional Council
Regional Buildings
Glenurquhart Road
Inverness IV3 5NX
Tel: 0463 234121

Yorkshire and Humberside Euro Info Centre
Westgate House, Wellington Street
Leeds LS1 4LT
Tel: 0532 439222

Euro Info Centre
30 New Walk
Leicester LE1 6TF
Tel: 0533 554464

North West Euro Service Ltd
Liverpool Central Libraries
William Brown Street
Liverpool L3 8EW
Tel: 051 298 1928

Small Firms Service
11 Belgrave Road
London SW1W 1RB
Tel: 071 248 4444

London Chamber of Commerce
69 Cannon Street
London SW1V 1RB
Tel: 071 828 6201

Kent County Council
Euro Info Centre
Springfield
Maidstone ME1 2LL
Tel: 0622 671411

Manchester Chamber of Commerce and Industry
Euro Info Centre
56 Oxford Street
Manchester M60 7HJ
Tel: 061 236 3210

Northern Development Company
Euro Info Centre
Bank House
Carliol Square
Newcastle-upon-Tyne NE1 6XE
Tel: 091 261 5131

Norwich and Norfolk Chamber of Commerce and Industry
Euro Info Centre
112 Barrack Street
Norwich NR3 1UB
Tel: 0603 625977

Nottinghamshire Chamber of Commerce and Industry
Euro Info Centre
Faraday Building
Highfield Science Park
Nottingham NG7 2QP
Tel: 0602 222414

Wales Euro Info Centre
University College Cardiff
PO Box 430
Cardiff CF1 3XT
Tel: 0222 874000 x6030

Thames Chiltern Chamber of Commerce
Commerce House
2–6 Bath Road
Slough, Berks SL1 3SB
Tel: 0753 77877

Shropshire Chamber of Commerce and Industry
Euro Info Centre
Industry House
16 Halesford, Telford
Shropshire TF7 4TA
Tel: 0952 588766

Southern Area Euro Info Centre
Central Library
Civic Centre
Southampton SO9 4XP
Tel: 0703 832866

European Documentation Centres

The primary function of the EDCs is to stimulate and sustain the development of the study of Europe in the academic institutions of the regions where they are based. In addition, they are requested, when circumstances permit, to provide an EC information service to the wider community.

EDC
Queen Mother Library
The University
Meston Walk
Aberdeen AB9 2UE
Tel: 0224 272000 x2587

The Library
Wye College
Ashford, Kent TN25 5AH
Tel: 0223 812401 x497

The Library
University of Bath
Claverton Down
Bath BA2 7AY
Tel: 0225 826826 x5594

EDC
Govt. Publications
Main Library
Queens University
Belfast BT7 1LS
Tel: 0232 245133 x3605

William Kendrick Library
Birmingham Polytechnic
Perry Barr
Birmingham B42 2SU
Tel: 021 331 5298

EDC
Main Library
University of Birmingham
PO Box 363
Birmingham B15 2TT
Tel: 021 414 5823

J. B. Priestley Library
University of Bradford
Richmond Road
Bradford BD7 1DP
Tel: 0274 383402

EDC
Documents Section
University of Sussex Library
Falmer, Brighton BN1 9QL
Tel: 0273 678159

University of Bristol
Wills Memorial Library
Queens Road
Bristol BS8 1RL
Tel: 0272 303370

The Library
University of Cambridge
Cambridge CB3 9DR
Tel: 0233 333138

EDC
Library Building
University of Kent at Canterbury
Canterbury CT2 7NU
Tel: 0227 764000 x3109

EDC
The Guest Building
UWCC, PO Box 430
Cardiff CF1 3XT
Tel: 0222 874262

Albert Sloman Library
University of Essex
PO Box 24
Wivenhoe Park
Colchester CO4 3UA
Tel: 0206 873333 x3181

EDC
University of Ulster
Cromor Road, Coleraine
Co. Londonderry BT52 1SA
Tel: 0265 44141 x4257

EDC
The Library
University of Warwick
Coventry CV4 7AL
Tel: 0203 523523 x2041

Lanchester Library
Coventry Polytechnic
Much Park Street
Coventry CV1 5HF
Tel: 0203 838452/698

EDC
Law Library
University of Dundee
Dundee DD1 4HN
Tel: 0382 23181 x4100

The Library
University of Durham
Stockton Road
Durham DH1 3LY
Tel: 091 374 3041/44

EDC
Europa Library
University of Edinburgh
Old College, South Bridge
Edinburgh EH8 9YL
Tel: 031 667 1011 x4292

Centre for European Legal Studies
University of Exeter
Amory Building
Rennes Drive
Exeter EH8 9YL
Tel: 0392 263356

University Library
University of Glasgow
Hillhead Street
Glasgow G12 8QE
Tel: 041 339 8855 x6744

George Edwards Library
University of Surrey
Guildford GU2 5XH
Tel: 0483 509233

Brynmor Jones Library
University of Hull
Cottingham Road
Hull HU6 7RX
Tel: 0482 465940

EDC
Keele University Library
Keele ST5 5BG
Tel: 0782 621111 x3738

The Library
University of Lancaster
Bailrigg, Lancaster LA1 4YX
Tel: 0524 65201 x2543

Leeds Polytechnic Library
Calverley Street
Leeds LS1 3HE
Tel: 0532 832600 x3280

Law Library
Lyddon Terrace
University of Leeds
Leeds LS2 9JT
Tel: 0532 335040/335312

The Library
University of Leicester
PO Box 248
University Road
Leicester LE1 9QD
Tel: 0533 522044

The Library
Queen Mary & Westfield College
Mile End Road
London E1 4NS
Tel: 071 975 5555 x3327

The Library
Polytechnic of North London
Prince of Wales Road
London NW5
Tel: 071 607 2789 x4110

The Library
Royal Institute of International Affairs
10 St James's Square
London SW1Y 4LE
Tel: 071 930 2233 x260

British Library of Political
and Economic Science
10 Portugal Street
London WC2A 2HD
Tel: 071 955 7273

Pilkington Library
Loughborough University of
Technology
Loughborough LE11 3TU
Tel: 0509 222344

John Rylands Library
University of Manchester
Oxford Road
Manchester M13 9PP
Tel: 061 275 3751

EDC
Polytechnic Library
Ellison Place
Newcastle-upon-Tyne NE1 8ST
Tel: 091 232 6002 x4136

The Library
University of East Anglia
University Plain
Norwich NR4 7TJ
Tel: 0603 56161 x2412

Hallward Library
University of Nottingham
Nottingham NG7 2RD
Tel: 0602 484848 x3741

EDC
Radcliffe Camera
Bodleian Library
Oxford OX1 3BG
Tel: 0865 277201

Frewen Library
Portsmouth Polytechnic
Cambridge Road
Portsmouth PO1 2ST
Tel: 0705 827681

The Library
University of Reading
Whiteknights, Reading RG6 2AE
Tel: 0734 318782

The Library
University of Salford
Salford M5 4WT
Tel: 061 736 5843 x7209

The Library
Sheffield City Polytechnic
Pond Street, Sheffield S1 1WB
Tel: 0742 532126

The Library
University of Southampton
Highfield, Southampton SO9 5NH
Tel: 0703 595000

The Robert Scott Library
The Polytechnic, St Peter's Square
Wolverhampton WV1 1RG
Tel: 0902 313005 x2300

DEPOSITORY LIBRARIES

Commercial and Social Sciences
Library
Central Libraries
William Brown Street
Liverpool L3 8EW
Tel: 051 207 2147

Westminster Central Reference
Library
35 St Martin's Street
London WC2H 7HP
Tel: 071 798 2034

British Library
Document Supply Centre
Boston Spa, Wetherby
W. Yorks LS23 7BQ
Tel: 0937 546044/546060

Bibliography

The European Community Fact Book
Alex Roney (Kogan Page)

Deadline 1992. Putting Europe to Work
(Commission of the European Communities Document)

Europe in Figures
(Eurostat Document)

Single European Act
(Bulletin of the European Communities – Supplement 2/86)

Europe without Frontiers – Completing the Internal Market
(European Communities Official Publications Office)

Europe – A Fresh Start. The Schuman Declaration 1950/1990
Pascal Fontaine (EC Official Publications Office)

European Unification – Gestation and Growth
(EC Official Publications Office)

The Single Market – The Facts
(Department of Trade and Industry Document)

EEC Competition Policy in the Single Market
(EC Official Publications Office)

The European Commission and the Administration of the Community
Richard Hay (EC Official Publications Office)

Freedom of Movement in the Community – Entry and Residence
Jean-Claude Séché (Commission of the European Communities Document)

A Guide to Working in a Europe without Frontiers
Jean-Claude Séché (Commission of the European Communities Document)

Employment in Europe
(Commission of the European Communities Document)

Finance from Europe
Dr Michael Hopkins (EC Official Publications Office)

Taxation in the Single Market
(EC Official Publications Office)

1992 – The Social Dimension
(EC Official Publications Office)

Campaign for a People's Europe
(Commission of the European Communities Document)

Vocational Education and the Challenge of Europe
Peter Funnel & Dave Müller (Kogan Page)

Britain and a Single Market Europe: Prospects for a Common School Curriculum
Martin McLean (Kogan Page)

Higher Education in the European Community – The Student Handbook
(Kogan Page)

Environmental Policy in the European Community
(European Community Publication)

A Common Agricultural Policy for the 1990s
(EC Official Publications Office)

The Audio-Visual Media in the Single European Market
Matteo Maggiore (Commission of the European Communities Document)

Commission of the European Communities Fact Sheets:
The Right to Work in a Member State of the EC
(Fact Sheet 2)
Social Security for Migrant Workers (FS 3)
Pensions and Retirement in the European Community (FS 4)
Europe for Students (FS 5)
Young People's Europe (FS 6)
Women's Rights and Opportunities (FS 7)
Mutual Recognition of Diplomas and Professional Qualifications
(FS 8)

T2 Leaflet: 'Health Advice for Travellers inside the European Community'
(Available at Post Offices or by calling Freephone 0880 555777)

Leaflet SA29: 'Your Social Security, Health Care and Pension Rights in the European Community'
(Department of Social Security)

Un Espace Social Européen à l'Horizon 1992
Patrick Venturini (Commission des Communautés Européennes)

Les Droits du Citoyen Européen
Georges-Henri Beauthier (Commission des Communautés Européennes)

Objectif 92 – Le Guide Pratique du Marché Unique
Bruno Vever (CNPF)

L'Europe 93 – Tout ce qui va Changer pour le Consommateur
Lindsay Armstrong & Alain Dauvergne (Balland)

Droit de Choisir et Impulsion Economique
Eamonn Lawlor (Commission des Communautés Européennes)

Un Espace Financier Européen
Dominique Servais (Commission des Communautés Européennes)

L'Europe Monétaire
Jean Pierre Patat (La Découverte)

Systèmes de Formation Professionnelle dans les Pays Membres de la CE – Etudes Comparatives
(Guide CEDEFOP)

Les Régions dans les Années 90 – Rapport périodique
(Commission des Communautés Européennes)

Europe 2000 – Les Perspectives de Développement du Territoire Communautaire. Document préliminaire
(Commission des Communautés Européennes)

La CEE et l'Environnement
(Observatoire Social Européen)

La Politique Européenne de l'Environnement
ENGREF (Romillat)

CE: Bilan Sanitaire de l'Etat des Forêts. 1989 Rapport de Synthèse
(Commission des Communautés Européennes)

Le Grand Marché Européen de 1993
Armand Bizaguet (PUF)

Le Marché Commun
Jean-François Deniau & Gérard Druesne (PUF)

Le Parlement Européen
Jean-Louis Burban & Pierre Ginestet (PUF)

Un Pari pour l'Europe
Michel Albert (Seuil)

La France par l'Europe
Jacques Delors & Clisthène (Grasset)

Euroscopie
Gérard Mermet (Larousse)

Portrait Social de l'Europe
(Document Eurostat)

Dossiers de l'Europe (Commission des Communautés Européennes):
   La Charte Communautaire des Droits Sociaux Fondamentaux des Travailleurs
   L'Education et la Formation à l'Horizon de 1992
   Le Budget de la Communauté Européenne
   Fiscalité et Coopération Transfrontalières des Entreprises
   Des Réseaux Transeuropéens dans une Communauté sans Frontières
   La Communauté Européenne et la Protection de l'Environnement

PERIODICAL PUBLICATIONS

DTI *Single Market News*
Le Monde Dossiers et Documents Avril 1991
  'Europe: l'Engrenage du Marché Unique'
7 Jours d'Europe (Weekly news bulletin)
(Commission des Communautés Européennes – Paris)
This Week in Europe (Weekly news-sheet)
(Commission of the European Communities – London)
L'Evènement Européen – Initiatives et Débats
'1992 et Après . . .'
'Eduquer en Europe'
Libération – Le Cahier Europe du Vendredi
Le Monde – Espace Européen

VIDEO CASSETTES

DTI Single Market Videos – Video Arts Production Ltd
(Aimed at businessmen, but informative and entertaining for everyone)
1992 – What's that?
(Winner of Fiction/Humour Award at Festival Euro 92)
Brussels, can you hear me?
Available from :   CFI Vision
                   PO Box 35
                   Wetherby
                   Yorkshire LS23 7EX
                   Tel: 0937 541010
                   Fax: 0937 541083

PUBLICATIONS ON THE EUROPEAN COMMUNITY ARE AVAILABLE AT:

HMSO Books
HMSO Publications Centre
51 Nine Elms Lane
London SW8 5DR
Tel: 071 873 9090
Fax: 071 873 8463

Alan Armstrong Ltd
2 Arkwright Road
Reading
Berks RG2 0SG
Tel: 0734 751855
Fax: 0734 755164

Index